THE COMEDY OF ERRORS
LOVE'S LABOUR'S LOST
& THE TWO GENTLEMEN OF VERONA

NOTES

including
- *Life of Shakespeare*
- *Introduction to Each Play*
- *List of Characters in Each Play*
- *Summaries and Commentaries for Each Play*
- *Selected Bibliography*

by
Denis Calandra, Ph.D.
Department of Theater
University of South Florida

Cliffs Notes
INCORPORATED
LINCOLN, NEBRASKA 68501

Editor

Gary Carey, M.A.
University of Colorado

Consulting Editor

James L. Roberts, Ph.D.
Department of English
University of Nebraska

ISBN 0-8220-0010-5
© Copyright 1982
by
C. K. Hillegass
All Rights Reserved
Printed in U.S.A.

1991 Printing

Cliffs Notes, Inc.   Lincoln, Nebraska

CONTENTS

The Two Gentlemen of Verona

LIFE OF SHAKESPEARE

Many books have assembled facts, reasonable suppositions, traditions, and speculations concerning the life and career of William Shakespeare. Taken as a whole, these materials give a rather comprehensive picture of England's foremost dramatic poet. Tradition and sober supposition are not necessarily false because they lack proved bases for their existence. It is important, however, that persons interested in Shakespeare should distinguish between *facts* and *beliefs* about his life.

From one point of view, modern scholars are fortunate to know as much as they do about a man of middle-class origin who left a small English country town and embarked on a professional career in sixteenth-century London. From another point of view, they know surprisingly little about the writer who has continued to influence the English language and its drama and poetry for more than three hundred years. Sparse and scattered as these facts of his life are, they are sufficient to prove that a man from Stratford by the name of William Shakespeare wrote the major portion of the thirty-seven plays which scholars ascribe to him. The concise review which follows will concern itself with some of these records.

No one knows the exact date of William Shakespeare's birth. His baptism occurred on Wednesday, April 26, 1564. His father was John Shakespeare, tanner, glover, dealer in grain, and town official of Stratford; his mother, Mary, was the daughter of Robert Arden, a prosperous gentleman-farmer. The Shakespeares lived on Henley Street.

Under a bond dated November 28, 1582, William Shakespeare and Anne Hathaway entered into a marriage contract. The baptism of their eldest child, Susanna, took place in Stratford in May, 1583. One year and nine months later their twins, Hamnet and Judith, were christened in the same church. The parents named them for the poet's friends Hamnet and Judith Sadler.

Early in 1596, William Shakespeare, in his father's name, applied to the College of Heralds for a coat of arms. Although positive proof is lacking, there is reason to believe that the Heralds granted this request, for in 1599 Shakespeare again made application for the right to quarter his coat of arms with that of his mother. Entitled to her father's coat of arms, Mary had lost this privilege when she married John Shakespeare before he held the official status of gentleman.

In May of 1597, Shakespeare purchased New Place, the outstanding residential property in Stratford at that time. Since John Shakespeare had suffered financial reverses prior to this date, William must have achieved success for himself.

Court records show that in 1601 or 1602, William Shakespeare began rooming in the household of Christopher Mountjoy in London. Subsequent disputes between Shakespeare's landlord, Mountjoy, and his son-in-law, Stephen Belott, over Stephen's wedding settlement led to a series of legal actions, and in 1612 the court scribe recorded Shakespeare's deposition of testimony relating to the case.

In July, 1605, William Shakespeare paid four hundred and forty pounds for the lease of a large portion of the tithes on certain real estate in and near Stratford. This was an arrangement whereby Shakespeare purchased half the annual tithes, or taxes, on certain agricultural products from sections of land in and near Stratford. In addition to receiving approximately ten percent income on his investment, he almost doubled his capital. This was possibly the most important and successful investment of his lifetime, and it paid a steady income for many years.

Shakespeare is next mentioned when John Combe, a resident of Stratford, died on July 12, 1614. To his friend, Combe bequeathed the sum of five pounds. These records and similar ones are important, not because of their economic significance but because they prove the existence of a William Shakespeare in Stratford and in London during this period.

On March 25, 1616, William Shakespeare revised his last will and testament. He died on April 23 of the same year. His body lies within the chancel and before the altar of the Stratford church. A rather wry inscription is carved upon his tombstone:

> Good Friend, for Jesus' sake, forbear
> To dig the dust enclosed here;
> Blest be the man that spares these stones
> And curst be he that moves my bones.

The last direct descendant of William Shakespeare was his granddaughter, Elizabeth Hall, who died in 1670.

These are the most outstanding facts about Shakespeare the man, as apart from those about the dramatist and poet. Such pieces of information, scattered from 1564 through 1616, declare the existence of such a person, not as a writer or actor, but as a private citizen. It is illogical to think that anyone would or could have fabricated these details for the purpose of deceiving later generations.

In similar fashion, the evidence establishing William Shakespeare as the foremost playwright of his day is positive and persuasive. Robert Greene's *Groatsworth of Wit*, in which he attacked Shakespeare, a mere actor, for presuming to write plays in competition with Greene and his fellow playwrights, was entered in the *Stationers' Register* on September 20, 1592. In 1594 Shakespeare acted before Queen Elizabeth, and in 1594 and 1595 his name appeared as one of the shareholders of the Lord Chamberlain's Company. Francis Meres in his *Palladis Tamia* (1598) called Shakespeare "mellifluous and hony-tongued" and compared his comedies and tragedies with those of Plautus and Seneca in excellence.

Shakespeare's continued association with Burbage's company is equally definite. His name appears as one of the owners of the Globe in 1599. On May 19, 1603, he and his fellow actors received a patent from James I designating them as the King's Men and making them Grooms of the Chamber. Late in 1608 or early in 1609, Shakespeare and his colleagues purchased the Blackfriars Theatre and began using it as their winter location when weather made production at the Globe inconvenient.

Other specific allusions to Shakespeare, to his acting and his writing, occur in numerous places. Put together, they form irrefutable testimony that William Shakespeare of Stratford and London was the leader among Elizabethan playwrights.

One of the most impressive of all proofs of Shakespeare's authorship of his plays is the First Folio of 1623, with the dedicatory verse which appeared in it. John Heminge and Henry Condell, members of Shakespeare's own company, stated that they collected and issued the plays as a memorial to their fellow actor. Many contemporary poets contributed eulogies to Shakespeare; one of the best known of these poems is by Ben Jonson, a fellow actor and, later, a friendly rival. Jonson also criticized Shakespeare's dramatic work in *Timber: or, Discoveries* (1641).

Certainly there are many things about Shakespeare's genius and career which the most diligent scholars do not know and cannot explain, but the facts which do exist are sufficient to establish Shakespeare's identity as a man and his authorship of the thirty-seven plays which reputable critics acknowledge to be his.

The Comedy of Errors

INTRODUCTION

This comedy is probably Shakespeare's earliest work. The play was first performed at Gray's Inn on December 28, 1594, as part of the Christmas festivities.

The plot was not original, of course. Shakespeare, like most other playwrights and authors of that time, based his work on another, earlier work. In Shakespeare's case, he chose one of Plautus's most highly respected comedies, the *Menaechmi*. Significantly, he did not rely exclusively on rhymed couplets for his comedy; in fact, half the play is in blank verse, an exceptional accomplishment for a beginning playwright.

The plot was well known to the public of the time. The use of mistaken identities, as well as the confusion of twins, had long been popular in the Western theater tradition. While Plautus had only one set of twins, Shakespeare has two; thus, in his comedy, he increases to a great extent the possibility of confusion. The comedy was a huge success then, and it has continued to be popular. Indeed, even Broadway audiences were ecstatic over a spectacular musical adaptation of *Comedy of Errors* in 1938, entitled *The Boys from Syracuse*.

To begin with, the plot situation seems hopeless (a melodramatic and romantic touch): a father has lost a son and a wife, and his remaining son has gone in search of his long-lost twin brother, and the desolate father has not heard from his remaining son for a long time; thus, he sets out in search of his son and, by accident, arrives in a city that is a sworn enemy to his own city. Accordingly, he faces almost certain death; yet, by the close of the play, the entire family – servants included – are reunited, and marriages are in the offing.

In addition, Shakespeare introduces the character of Luciana, a foil-sister of the fiercely jealous Adriana. She, in turn, furnishes the love interest for Antipholus of Syracuse. As a result, even in this, Shakespeare's first attempt at satisfying the seasoned Elizabethan theater-goers with a sparkling comedy, is a vivid demonstration of both a high degree of genius and creativity in this young playwright.

He combines adventure, the comedy of human folly, romance, and suspense in a play that while not one of his masterpieces can be said to be both clever and original and still popular today.

BRIEF SYNOPSIS

A merchant of Syracuse, Egeon, suffered a shipwreck some years ago in which he was separated from his wife, Emilia, from one of his twin sons, later Antipholus of Ephesus, and the son's slave, Dromio of Ephesus. The other slave's twin, Dromio of Syracuse and Egeon's remaining son, Antipholus of Syracuse, remained with Egeon. When he came of age, Antipholus of Syracuse was allowed to go in search of his lost brother. After a period of time, Egeon then set out after his remaining son, and the play begins as we learn of Egeon's capture and his condemnation to death by Duke Solinus in the hostile city of Ephesus. The details of Egeon's story move Solinus to pity, and he grants a reprieve until nightfall, by which time a ransom of a thousand marks must be raised.

The twists of plot arise when Antipholus of Syracuse arrives with his slave in Ephesus, where Antipholus's twin brother, together with his wife Adriana and their twin slave reside. Confusion mounts upon confusion: Antipholus of Syracuse abuses Dromio of Ephesus for nagging him to go home for dinner; Adriana locks her real husband out of their home because she takes the Syracusan twin for the Ephesian: it is the other Dromio's turn now to be beaten; Antipholus of Ephesus refuses to pay for a gold chain he had ordered (it was delivered to his brother) and so is arrested. As the situation grows more and more bewildering with everyone certain that everyone else is totally mad, the moment for Egeon's execution is quickly approaching. Antipholus of Ephesus demands that the Duke intercede for him. Egeon sees his son as a last minute savior, but is of course not recognized by him. In the end, the Syracusan twins emerge from an abbey where they had taken refuge, and the complications are resolved. The Abbess, who turns out to be Egeon's long-lost wife Emilia, invites them all at the end to discuss this "one day's error" and "make full satisfaction."

LIST OF CHARACTERS

Solinus, Duke of Ephesus

Because of the enmity between his city and Syracuse, Solinus arrests Egeon and condemns him to death at the start of the play. Moved to pity at hearing the Syracusan merchant's story, however, he grants a stay of execution. Solinus functions mainly as a sympathetic ear, allowing Egeon's story to be told to set the background for the farce.

Egeon, A Merchant of Syracuse

Egeon's bad luck generates the action of the play. A shipwreck split up his family in the distant past, and the present dramatic action shows the incredible events in the one-day process of reunion. Egeon's deepest despair at the loss of his family, and possibly his own life, reverses itself in the waning moments of the play.

Antipholus of Ephesus

The first "lost" son of Egeon; this Antipholus witnesses his secure home ground dissolve around him when, unbeknownst to him, his twin brother arrives in Ephesus. Even his wife seems part of a conspiracy to drive him mad.

Antipholus of Syracuse

The second twin, the "lost" son; he arrives in Ephesus in his quest to recover his scattered family only to find himself spellbound, as he sees it, in a city of witchcraft and trickery.

The Two Dromios

Exact look-alikes and slaves to the respective twin Antipholuses; the Dromios parallel exactly their masters' dilemmas and take regular beatings when the confusion of events bears too hard upon them.

Adriana

The attractive wife of Antipholus of Ephesus; she mistakenly welcomes his twin brother as her husband, much to her husband's dismay and the visitor's amazement.

Emilia

The long-lost wife of Egeon; she has become an Abbess at Ephesus. She offers refuge to her Syracusan son without knowing who he is, then at the end of the play, she invites the entire cast of characters to feast and discuss the day's events.

Angelo

An Ephesian goldsmith; he is drawn into the complications when he delivers a gold chain – ordered by one of the twins – to the other twin, and when he tries to collect payment from the first one.

Doctor Pinch

This quack proto-psychiatrist, called a "schoolmaster" by Shakespeare in his List of Characters, administers to Antipholus of Ephesus by suggesting that he and his slave be bound and laid in some dark room to exorcise the "fiend" within them. He is the only one of the characters left out of the happy resolution at the end of the play.

Luciana

Adriana's sister; she tries her best to calm Adriana at points of stress in the plot, but she too gets caught up in the enveloping madness. Shakespeare neatly pairs her off with Antipholus of Syracuse at the end of the play.

Balthazar

A merchant.

Luce

Adriana's servant.

SUMMARIES AND COMMENTARIES

ACT I – SCENE 1

Summary

The play's opening lines signal a mood of tension, and they portend disaster for Egeon, a middle-aged merchant from the ancient city of Syracuse on the island of Sicily. He tells his captor,

Proceed, Solinus, to procure my fall,
And by the doom of death end woes and all.
(1-2)

The cities of Syracuse and Ephesus are openly hostile toward one another. Captured in Ephesus, Egeon has been condemned to death by the Duke, who urges him to tell the sad story of how he has come to this state. Thus, Shakespeare sets the background for the play.

Along with his wife Emilia, identical twin sons both named Antipholus, and identical twin slaves both named Dromio, Egeon some years ago suffered a shipwreck. One son and slave survived with the father; the others, he hoped, survived with the mother. Neither group knew of the other's survival, however, nor of their whereabouts, but when Antipholus of Syracuse ("Egeon's twin" son) turned eighteen, his father gave him permission to search for his brother. The worried Egeon then set out after his *second* son, and after five years of fruitless wandering, he came to Ephesus. Moved by this tale of woe, the Duke of Ephesus gives his captive a day's reprieve, within which time Egeon must raise a "thousand marks" ransom money:

Try all the friends thou hast in Ephesus;
Beg thou, or borrow, to make up the sum,
And live; if no, then thou art doomed to die.
(153-55)

Commentary

The first scene of *Comedy of Errors* gives all the necessary details for understanding the complications of plot which are to follow. In addition, it sets the gloomy mood which, in keeping with the simple movement of one type of comedy, will give way to joy at the end of the play. Since Shakespeare constructs his plays as symphonies of mood, it should be kept in mind that this scene is not *mere* exposition of plot detail. "Hapless Egeon," in a deep state of depression, so affects the Duke of Ephesus that the latter is transformed from being a strict upholder of the letter of the law (". . . if any Syracusian born/Come to the bay of Ephesus, he dies") to someone who can say he only wishes it were in his power to help: "My soul should sue as advocate for thee." Lines like the following, depicting the shipwreck, touch the Duke's sensibility:

> For what obscured light the heavens did grant
> Did but convey unto our fearful minds
> A doubtful warrant of immediate death,
> Which, though myself would gladly have embraced,
> Yet the incessant weepings of my wife,
> Weeping before for what she saw must come,
> And piteous plainings of the pretty babes,
> That mourned for fashion, ignorant what to fear,
> Forced me to seek delays for them and me.
>
> (67-75)

That "delay" ended in disaster, as Egeon sees it; small wonder that the "delay" granted him by the Duke at the end of the scene does not stir much hope.

ACT I – SCENE 2

Summary

Antipholus of Syracuse (hereafter referred to as Antipholus of S.) takes his leave of a friendly merchant and bids his servant Dromio of S. to take the 1,000 marks he has with him to their lodgings for safekeeping. Meanwhile, he says, he'll "view the manners of the town" and "go lose myself." The plot complications develop immediately as Dromio of E., an exact look-alike of the other Dromio, enters and bids Antipholus of S., thinking of course that he is Antipholus of E., to come home for dinner for "the clock hath strucken twelve" and "your worship's wife" has been kept waiting. In no mood for dilly-dallying with a mischievous servant, Antipholus thumps the uncomprehending Dromio about the head, and as he runs off, Antipholus groans with the "knowledge" that he has been cheated out of 1,000 marks by a wily bondsman.

Commentary

As scene 1 strikes a chord of gloom to open the comedy, scene 2 introduces a sense of disorientation and confusion. Like his father, Antipholus of S. is near despair of ever finding his brother and mother:

> I to the world am like a drop of water
> That in the ocean seeks another drop.

> (33-34)

Several times he speaks of "losing himself," and with the first comical (to the audience) mistaking of servants, he seems to have lost his financial security as well. Ephesus has a reputation for strange goings-on:

> They say this town is full of cozenage:
> As nimble jugglers that deceive the eye,
> Dark-working sorcerers that change the mind,
> Soul-killing witches that deform the body,
> Disguised cheaters. . . .

> (96-100)

and Shakespeare will make much in the course of the play of bizarre, dream-like effects apparently brought on by pure chance.

ACT II – SCENE 1

Summary

Antipholus of E.'s wife, Adriana, debates with her sister Luciana on the proper conduct of authority in marriage. Luciana's conventional (Renaissance) wisdom that men "are masters to their females, and their lords" meets with Adriana's skepticism: easy enough to talk about a man's rightful liberty when you are not married yourself, she says. Dromio breaks up the conversation with the complaint that his master has just given him a cuffing ("he's at two hands with me") and demanded the return of a "nonexistent" thousand marks. The servant's report of his master's words, "I know no house, no wife, no mistress," sends Adriana into a fit of anger, causing her sister to comment, "How many fond fools serve mad jealousy!"

Commentary

Even the secondary characters are unhappy when the plot gets under way. A constant theme in Shakespeare's comedies is the question of harmony between the sexes, here invoked in minor fashion in his first play. The idea of "mastery" and "liberty" in *Comedy of Errors*, whether it be husband/wife or master/servant is not so important in itself as it is as part of a general context of man's (and woman's) mastery over his (or her) own fate. Beginning with Nature's surrealist joke (identical twins), *Comedy of Errors* for the most part light-heartedly explores ways in which people are caught up in webs spun according to the laws of chance. This, of course, is one primal appeal of farce: natural repetition and duplication – when compounded to include individuals themselves – threatening even their senses of identity, can be frightening. The pain on stage can be very real. The following exchange from the next scene sums up the point:

> *Antipholus of S.:* Dost thou not know?
> *Dromio of S.:*   Nothing sir, but that I am
>   beaten. . . .
> Was there ever any man thus
>   beaten out of season,
> When in the Why and the Where-
>   fore is neither rhyme nor
>   reason?
>   (II, ii, 41-49)

ACT II – SCENE 2

Summary

Antipholus of S. beats Dromio of S., this time, for his former "insolence," warning him in the future to be sure *precisely* when the time is right for jesting ("Know my aspect"). Dromio takes the beating, completely ignorant about the reason for it, after which the two engage in witty dialogue about Time.

When Adriana and Luciana enter, taking the Syracusan Antipholus for the Ephesian, the two men begin to doubt their senses.

> *Dromio:* I am transformed, master, am not I?
> *Antipholus:* I think thou art in mind, and so am I.
>
> (198-99)

Their bewilderment follows quickly upon Adriana's long forgiving speech to her "husband." Antipholus of S. correctly explains that he has only been in Ephesus for two hours, and therefore he does not know who Adriana is. When Luciana recounts having sent Dromio (of E.) to fetch him to dinner, Antipholus of S. becomes further befuddled, suspecting that *his* servant is in on a practical joke. By the end of the scene, however, both master and servant simply agree to play along with the (rather pleasant) madness of going to dinner with a beautiful woman who thinks she is wife and mistress to them.

> *Antipholus of S.* [aside]:
> Am I in earth, in heaven, or in hell?
> Sleeping or waking, made or well-advised?
> Known unto these, and to myself disguised?
> I'll say as they say, and persever so,
> And in this mist at all adventures go.
>
> (214-18)

Commentary

Master and servant begin the scene at odds with one another, and by its end they are jointly subject to one of the plot's "errors," this time taken as a potentially enjoyable spell to which they may just voluntarily surrender themselves. In the middle of the scene, the two of them banter on the topic of Time, a favorite theme of Shakespeare's. Note the numerous references to Time and Time passing up to this point in the play, and note the effect of the speed-up action of the farce as the play proceeds. Antipholus of S. has been in Ephesus two hours and has already despaired of finding his family, has been "bereft" of his money, has had to beat "his" servant twice, has been invited to a private dinner in an upstairs chamber by an enchanting stranger (though he prefers her sister), and there is more to come. On stage all this has transpired very quickly, drawing the audience into the illusion of the whirl of events. "Was I married to her in my dreams?" Antipholus of S. asks himself, thus extending the real vs. waking time theme to the hours when one lives at a subconscious level.

ACT III – SCENE 1

Summary

Antipholus of Ephesus, together with his servant, a goldsmith, and the merchant Balthazar, try to gain entry to his home but are refused entry by Dromio of S:

Either get thee from the door or sit down at the hatch.
Dost thou conjure for wenches?

(33-34)

At Balthazar's warning that too much tumult outside his home may endanger Antipholus of E.'s reputation (by drawing his wife's honor into question), the group moves on. Antipholus is determined "to spite [his] wife," so he stalks off to the Porpentine Inn where he knows "a wench of excellent discourse."

Commentary

This scene introduces Antipholus of Ephesus, who has considerably fewer lines in the play than his twin. For him, the "errors" so far are not quite as dislocating as for his brother, since he has not been traveling for years and is in his home environment. Shakespeare changed the orientation of the plot of *Comedy of Errors* from its source, the 2nd century B.C. Roman comedy by Plautus, the *Menaechmi*, in this respect. He wished to convey the opening of the play from the point of view of the strangers in this strange land, thus underscoring his theme of total bewilderment brought about by *chance* aspects of life. Antipholus of E. is moved only to seek revenge in a domestic squabble, his remark on the occasion being the relatively mild: "There is something in the wind."

ACT III — SCENE 2

Summary

Luciana entreats Antipholus of S. to be kind to his "wife," even if he must be a hypocrite in the process. "Alas, poor woman!" she exclaims:

> Make us but believe,
> Being compact of credit, that you love us;
> Though others have the arm, show us the sleeve.
>
> (21-23)

He shocks Luciana by his response—that he loathes Adriana and deeply loves her: "Far more, far more to you do I decline [incline]." When Luciana runs off, Dromio of S. enters to explain that he too is having problems with a member of the opposite sex: "She's the kitchen wench, and all grease." Master and servant, truly worried that witchcraft is involved, determine to set forth on the first available ship.

Compounding matters at the end of the scene is Angelo the goldsmith, who delivers a gold chain to Antipholus of S., which he "ordered" for his wife. Antipholus of S. refuses payment, saying they can settle later.

Commentary

Antipholus of S. grows more confused as his emotional involvement with the sister of the woman who claims to be his wife becomes greater. In one of the few lyrical passages in the play, he woos the bemused Luciana:

> O, train me not, sweet mermaid, with thy note,
> To drown me in thy sister's flood of tears.
>
> (45-46)

In contrast to this, Dromio outlines the hideous features of the kitchen maid's anatomy in geographical terms. Shakespeare's only direct reference to America in any of his plays appears here:

> *Antipholus of S*: Where America, the Indies?
> *Dromio of S*: O, sir, upon her nose, all o'er

embellished with rubies, carbuncles, sapphires,
declining their rich aspect to the hot breath of
Spain, who sent whole armadoes or caracks
[ships] to be ballast [loaded] at her nose.

(137-40)

There ought to be a sense of dread from the two characters on stage
when they realize that witchcraft may be involved. The audience, of
course, aware that the danger is not real, can enjoy the hubbub all
the more (" 'Tis time, I think, to trudge, pack, and be gone. . . . I'll
stop mine ears against the mermaid's song.").

ACT IV – SCENE 1

Summary

A merchant anxious to go on a business voyage entreats Angelo
to pay a debt he owes, but Angelo cannot pay until five o'clock when
Antipholus is to give him the money for his gold chain. At that moment Antipholus of E. enters with his servant, Dromio, whom he
discharges to go buy a whip with which he plans to chastise his "wife
and her confederates." Antipholus of E. had ordered the gold chain,
but as we saw in the previous scene it was Antipholus of S. who
received it. With the merchant anxious to depart ("The hour steals
on"), tempers rise at the confusion. The upshot is two arrests: Angelo
for non-payment of debt, and Antipholus of E. for refusal to pay for
his gold chain. Adding further to the luancy is Dromio of S., who arrives to tell Antipholus of E. that he has booked passage for himself
and his master on a "bark of Epidamnum," scheduled to leave
shortly. This naturally casts further suspicion onto Antipholus of E.
Dromio of S. then thinks his master is mad when he is told to return
home (i.e., to Adriana) and fetch a "purse of ducats" for bail money.
He goes, however:

Thither I must, although against my will;
For servants must their masters' minds fulfill.

(112-13)

Commentary

The urgency of time presses on the action in this scene, as the
comings and goings speed up in the presence of a merchant feverishly

trying to collect his bills. Antipholus of E. is drawn into the "serious"
plot because he is under arrest by the end of scene 1. His quickness to
judge and to punish (preparing to flog his wife) at the start of the scene
contrasts comically with his predicament at the end. Note the tone of
Dromio of S.'s lines quoted above: it is as if he is becoming accustomed
to the lunatic twists of circumstances and of the whims of his "master."
Abnormal behavior threatens gradually to establish itself as the norm.

ACT IV – SCENE 2

Summary

Luciana tells Adriana of Antipholus's strange behavior toward her,
which sets off another jealous tirade: "He is deformed, crooked, old
and sere." Her tune soon changes though, revealing her true feelings:
"My heart prays for him, though my tongue do curse." When Dromio
of S. arrives to beg bail money for his master, Adriana complies.

Commentary

As the action briskly moves forward, Shakespeare has Dromio
deliver a short speech on the theme of Time, which the servant
wishes would reverse itself for the sake of his master:

> Time is a very bankrupt and owes more than he's
>   worth to season.
> Nay, he's a thief too; have you not heard men say,
> That Time comes stealing on by night and day?
> If 'a be in debt and theft, and a sergeant in the way,
> Hath he not reason to turn back an hour in a day?
> (57-61)

Compare these lines from Shakespeare's first play, a piece with all
the fever and the frenetic excitement of youth, with Macbeth's
famous comment on Time as he faces his last hours:

> Tomorrow, and tomorrow, and tomorrow.
> Creeps in this petty pace from day to day . . .

In reading Shakespeare, it is useful to look at his works as a whole to
see the development of the dramatist as he transforms the common-

22

place ideas of his age (here, that life is short) into concrete poetical realities. Note also that both in his comedies and his tragedies, Shakespeare incorporates his theme of the brevity of life, as well as the rush of confused time into the theatrical fact of actors strutting and fretting away their hours upon the stage. The action of *Comedy of Errors* on stage must be at breakneck speed, rather like the last reel of a Marx brothers film.

ACT IV – SCENE 3

Summary

Antipholus of S., alone on stage, recounts each strange occurrence of the day, concluding that "Lapland sorcerers" must inhabit the place. Just as he lists the last bit of madness, in comes Dromio of S. with the gold for bail money which his master had demanded that he fetch. Antipholus of S., knowing nothing of his own "arrest" grows acutely bewildered:

> The fellow is distract, and so am I,
> And here we wander in illusions.
> Some blessed power deliver us from hence!
>
> (42-44)

When a courtesan arrives requesting a gold chain in exchange for a ring which she claims to have given Antipholus, he takes her to be the devil incarnate, and he exits post-haste. The courtesan concludes that he must be mad and decides to tell his wife that he had stolen her ring by force.

Commentary

Two points should be made about this scene. First, try to envision two good actors playing the parts of Dromio and Antipholus. As characters, the two of them enjoy "playing" with and for each other: they exchange witty remarks, feign arguments, and sometimes go too far with their "performances," which usually result in the master thumping the servant. This conventional relationship between well-bred masters and their servants in Shakespeare's comedy also exists in the Roman play which he used as a model. In Shakespeare's comedies, the fools (and servants) have a certain degree of freedom with their masters, which is denied to other people, but they must always be careful not to break the unwritten code, not to overstep their bounds. We have noticed the comedy of the early scenes when Antipholus of S. beats Dromio of E. because of the "joke," as he saw it, about a wife waiting to share dinner with him. The beating came quickly then. Here, one must imagine Dromio of S. taking pause when his "master" denies knowing anything about bail money, but pursuing the matter and simultaneously feeling him out to see if he is "playing" a game. Accustomed to his master's whimsical, abnormal behavior by now, Dromio seems to carry on the game when Antipholus of S. remains serious. This is evident in Antipholus's quite serious fear of the witch, in the image of a courtesan, and Dromio's continued banter through the whole exchange: "Marry, he must have a long spoon that must eat with the devil."

The second matter of note in this scene is the biblical cast of the language. Though the comedy brought on by the errors is paramount, the fact that Shakespeare has his sympathetic character Antipholus appear beside himself and use Christ's words to the devil who tempted Him in the desert ("Satan, avoid!" – equivalent to "Get thee behind me, Satan") indicates that at one level the fear is real and the affair serious. If dreams and the subconscious are one source of other non-rational realities, another source very real to the Elizabethans was the nether world of demons and their legions of witches. *Comedy of Errors* is farce, but one of the chief appeals of farce can be its invitation to audiences to release themselves through laughter from deep-lying fears and the sneaking suspicion that a combination of pure chance, sheer chaos at the heart of things, or alternately but no more comfortingly, malevolent forces control our destinies. In Shakespeare's late plays, these themes are developed elaborately; their sketchy presence here, however, should not be overlooked if one is to capture the sense of this early work.

ACT IV – SCENE 4

Summary

Antipholus of Ephesus is at the center of this scene. First, he is told by Dromio of Ephesus that he has fetched the flogging rope, but has no memory of being asked to collect five hundred ducats bail money. Antipholus uses the whip on Dromio, who groans in response:

> I have served him from the hour of my nativity to this instant, and have nothing at his hands for my service but blows.
>
> (31-33)

Adriana enters with a schoolmaster, Doctor Pinch, who is to treat her husband for demonic possession:

> I charge thee, Satan, housed within this man,
> To yield possession to my holy prayers . . . .
>
> (57-58)

When Dromio of E. corroborates Antipholus of E.'s story that Adriana had locked them out earlier, she takes it as a ruse to soothe her poor mad husband. Dromio of E. probably thinks *she* is crazy; meanwhile, the doctor orders the two of them be treated in the accepted Elizabethan manner for dealing with the insane: "They must be bound and laid in some dark room." A battle-royal ensues, with Dr. Pinch blustering on about the "fiend" being "strong within him," Antipholus fighting for his life, and Luciana trying to smooth the troubled waters. Finally, Adriana promises to make good for the outstanding debt, and Antipholus of E., together with his Dromio, are led off by the doctor and others.

Before poor Adriana has had time to catch her breath, her "husband" and his servant return. It is Antipholus of S. and Dromio of S.:

> *Luciana:* God, for thy mercy! they are loose again.
> *Adriana:* And come with naked [drawn] swords.
> Let's call more help to have them bound
> again.
> *Officer:* Away! they'll kill us!
> (Exit, "as fast as may be.")
>
> (147-51)

Though Dromio of S. feels that "they will surely do us no harm," Antipholus is determined to leave the city at once.

Commentary

Groucho Marx once said that real comedy depends on a sense of its opposite for full effect: when an old lady in a wheelchair is shoved down a flight of stairs in a comedy, you hold your breath as she approaches the brick wall at the bottom, and when a ramp miraculously appears at the last possible instant gliding her to safety on the other side, the laughter you experience is inseparable from relief at disaster cheated of its due. Without the brick wall, however, the effect would not be the same. Sigmund Freud and numerous other eminent thinkers have remarked on the same phenomenon as Groucho. This scene and the next are Shakespeare's "brick wall" scenes in *Comedy of Errors*. The mistaken identities have reached the stage where physical harm may come to the innocent participants; we have: Dr. Pinch, a mad proto-psychiatrist; a raging Antipholus; a pitying wife; and sword-bearing "doubles" threatening each other with physical and mental harm. The measure of comedy here, and the speed of the scene, which begins with a flogging and ends with a quick escape, is at its most frenetically enjoyable. Whatever *can* go wrong, it seems, *does*. Dromio of S., at the end of the scene, surely to the horror of his master, is even tempted to give in to the frenzy in the air (it hasn't done too much harm to him yet) and join the "demons": "Methinks they are such a gentle nation that, but for the mountain of mad flesh that claims marriage of me, I could find in my heart to stay here still [forever] and turn witch."

ACT V – SCENE 1

Summary

While Angelo the goldsmith explains his predicament to another merchant and explains that Antipholus (normally "of very reverend reputation") has the gold chain, Antipholus of S. and his Dromio enter. Antipholus wears the chain, feels himself defiled as a "villain" by the merchant and Angelo, who accuse him of non-payment, and he prepares to engage in a swordfight to secure his honor. Adriana intercedes when she enters, allowing Antipholus of S. and Dromio of S. to seek refuge in a priory.

The Abbess of the priory calms Adriana, who wants to recapture her "insane" husband and bind him for his own good. In contrast to

Dr. Pinch of the previous scene, the Abbess is a sensitive person with the interest of the men seeking sanctuary at heart. She inquires about Adriana's behavior and her husband's behavior, concluding:

> And thereof came it that the man was mad.
> The venom clamors of a jealous woman
> Poisons more deadly than a mad dog's tooth.
>
> (68-70)

The Abbess takes it as "a charitable duty of my order" to try to succor Antipholus. Adriana squabbles:

> And ill it doth beseem your holiness
> To separate the husband and the wife.
>
> (110-11)

When the Duke enters on his way with Egeon to "the place of death and sorry execution" where he is to be "beheaded publicly," Adriana pleads with him to force the Abbess to relinquish her "mad" husband.

The confusion compounds itself steadily as a messenger arrives to announce Antipholus's escape *in another part of town*, where:
> My master and his man are both broke loose,
> Beaten the maids a-row [in a row], and bound the doctor,
> Whose beard they have singed off with brands of fire,
> And ever [even] as it blazed, they threw on him
> Great pails of puddled mire to quench the hair.
>
> (169-73)

Adriana is near hysteria as she hears her "husband's" cry at this very moment within the abbey. She thinks she must be possessed:

> Ay me, it is my husband! Witness you,
> That he is borne about invisible.
>
> (186-87)

Inevitably, Antipholus of Ephesus next enters, begging help from his lord and former commander in battle ("[I] took/Deep scars to save thy life."). All of the facts come to light, as Antipholus of E. describes what has happened (and has *not* happened, though others think it has) to him this day. The crowd of onlookers can and cannot cor-

roborate what he says. The Duke sums up the situation pointedly –
"Why, this is strange" – before he sends for the Abbess.

Egeon first sees his salvation at "the eleventh hour" (in this case,
when "the dial points at five") in the person of his son, only to have
his despair redoubled when Antipholus of E. denies ever having set
eyes on him.

> Not know my voice! O, time's extremity,
> Hast thou so cracked and splitted my poor tongue
> In seven short years, that here my only son
> Knows not my feeble key [voice] of untuned cares?
> (305-8)

The Duke takes Egeon at this juncture for a senile and sorrow-crazed
old man: "thy eye and dangers make thee dote."

The recognition scene ends the play as the Abbess, Antipholus of
S., and Dromio of S. make their entry much to the amazement of all
at hand. After the formal recognitions, the Abbess bids them retire:

> And hear at large discoursèd all our fortunes;
> And all that are assembled in this place,
> That by this sympathizèd [shared] one day's error.
> Have suffered wrong, go, keep us company,
> And we shall make full satisfaction.
> (394-98)

Commentary

The disentanglement is rapid, adding to the wonder of the comedy. Egeon's despair deepens before he is redeemed. In the Duke's
comment on Egeon's "dotage," Shakespeare is referring to yet another
aspect of time and perception: with old age, a special state of con-
sciousness, parallel to "dreams" or "possession," arrives in the form of
senility. All of the characters in the play are spellbound by the turn
of events, as the entire saga of Egeon's family comes to a happy ending. The only character left out of the euphoria is the quack, Dr.
Pinch. The spirit of most of Shakespeare's comedies is joyful at the
end, and his first effort is no exception. The just pairings of members
of the opposite sex which occupy the last moments of his comedies is
not given great emphasis here, though it is clear that the Abbess
(Emilia) and Egeon, Antipholus of E. and Adriana, and Antipholus of

S. and Luciana are all bound to one another. As a last, brilliant, light touch, Shakespeare allows the confusions to linger on as the Duke says to the Antipholus pair, "Stay, stand apart; I know not which is which," and the two Dromio's are left on stage vying for seniority rights among slaves. They decide to decide, appropriately, according to the laws of chance which got them into the fix in the first place: "We'll draw cuts for the senior," says Dromio of Syracuse . . . or is it Dromio of Ephesus?

Love's Labour's Lost

INTRODUCTION

Most scholars believe that this play was authored by Shakespeare, produced, and then revised and rewritten by Shakespeare for later performances. In one of the earliest references to the play, in the quarto of 1598, we find *Love's Labour's Lost* being referred to as "a pleasant comedy"; furthermore, we read that it was "presented before her Highness this last Christmas. Newly corrected and augmented by W. Shakespeare." What we have, then, is, really, a revised version of a play that Shakespeare felt needed additional work. That is, he was not content with it, and he was not merely correcting it as a proofreader might, but he was correcting it as a playwright would, for he was interested in the dramatic dimensions and worth of the play and not in its *printed* text. This fact is obvious if one studies the folio itself, for it is filled with textual ambiguities. Each editor of a Shakespeare collection has a true task before him when he confronts this play and must decide on a "text" that he considers both accurate and "genuine."

Curiously, Shakespeare apparently used no known source for this play, and thus scholars have concentrated, most often, on various similarities between this play's focus on sonnet writing and the sonnets which Shakespeare was composing at approximately the same time that he wrote this play.

In the eighteenth century, *Love's Labour's Lost* was perhaps the most unpopular of all of Shakespeare's plays, and even in the nineteenth century, it was held in low esteem. While the play is not one of Shakespeare's most mature comedies, modern audiences who are familiar with *Romeo and Juliet* can appreciate Shakespeare's irony and satire as he scoffs at lovers "in love with love," rather than in love with a woman. This comedy is filled with duplicity and poseurs — much like the early Romeo, who fancied himself "deathly" in love with Rosaline, a character who never appears in the play — appropriately because her significance is more in Romeo's imagination than in reality.

Shakespeare's satiric sense which he was to use throughout the rest of his life is first evidenced here. Yet, in this early play, one does not feel that the satire is forced or bitter; it is fresh, it has a free and easy quality, and, most of all, it is playful. Some Shakespeare scholars believe that Shakespeare was attacking a certain group of intellectuals who considered themselves elitely studious; the group included Sir Walter Raleigh and the poet Thomas Nashe, among others. If this *is* true, however, Shakespeare was not "attacking" them; the flavor that flows throughout this comedy is merry, and its plea is for simplicity and common sense. If anything, Shakespeare was satirizing excess — in all its varieties. The quality in human beings which Shakespeare valued highly and which he evokes here is *mirth*. He places himself at a distance from humankind and invites us to do the same and laugh at our follies.

Shakespeare focuses on two subjects — the folly which lovers fall prey to and the sonnets which they write to their beloveds. Sonnet writing was in fashion when this play was written, and a lighthearted satire on this fad was a sure-fire formula for a light evening's entertainment for the very learned Queen Elizabeth I and her court. There *is* some historical basis for the sketchy plot, however; Shakespeare did not make up a pretense of a framework on which to hang his satire. In 1578, Catherine de Medici of France (along with her daughter, Marguerite, and a number of ladies-in-waiting) did sail to the court of Henry of Navarre in order to try and arrange for the final sovereignty of the Aquitane to be decided. Shakespeare, however, does not dwell seriously on this framework. He merely uses it as a backdrop against which to present his comedy.

Perhaps it should be noted here that Shakespeare does not use entirely original comic characters in this play, even though he used no known comedy "source." For example, he borrows certain "types" from the Italian *commedia dell'arte*. He includes the loud braggart (Armado), a type that appears in drama as early as Plautus's stylized *miles gloriosus*. Then there is also the zany (Moth), the pedant (Holofernes), the parasite (Nathaniel), the stupid rustic (Costard), and the unlearned magistrate (Dull). These were enduring types which also appeared on French and German stages and would eventually find their way into comic operas.

BRIEF SYNOPSIS

The King of Navarre and his followers, Biron, Longaville, and Dumain, vow to devote themselves to the celibate life of scholarship for three years. Their counterparts, the Princess of France and her attendant ladies, Rosaline, Maria, and Katherine, are refused entry to the city when they arrive, and therefore they decide to force the men to break their vows. Each of the men in his turn falls prey to the charms of the ladies and rationalizes his change of heart in the cleverest academic rhetoric he can write into a sonnet.

The ladies do not allow themselves to be taken so easily, however. When the gentlemen disguise themselves and pursue them as Russians in an elaborate courtly masque, the ladies confuse them by donning disguises also. The entire company engages in an extended exchange of witticisms while they prepare to watch a show prepared by the subplot characters, all of whom echo the concerns of the main characters in various ways. The entertainments are cut short by the announcement of the Princess's father's death, and a period of one year's abstinence is imposed on the men before they will be allowed to consummate their loves.

The comic subplot concerns the "fantastical" Spaniard Don Armado in pursuit of the country girl Jaquenetta. His rival in love is the "clown" Costard, and together with a pedantical schoolmaster, Holofernes, and his associate, Nathaniel, they all present a garbled burlesque of classical material at the end of the play.

LIST OF CHARACTERS

Ferdinand, King of Navarre

The King of Navarre wishes to turn his court into "a little Academe," to which end he elicits a vow from his closest followers to remain with him for three years as celibate scholars. Like his friends, however, the king soon finds the vow impossible to keep, especially when he meets the beautiful daughter of the King of France. Cupid is revenged, and to do penance for his actions at the end of the play, Navarre must wait for a year before he is allowed to be united with his beloved.

Biron

Biron is the most outspoken of the king's followers, the one who first expresses reservations about Navarre's scheme; he sees through the hypocrisy of his friends' vows. He reluctantly agrees to take the vow, and, like them, he eventually breaks it.

Longaville and Dumain

Navarre's other two attendant lords; the first to pledge chastity and the first to fall.

Boyet

An elderly lord attending the Princess of France; he acts as advisor and go-between.

Princess of France

The Princess has been sent by her father to Navarre to negotiate a debt owed for past years. Navarre retains possession of Aquitane, to the consternation of the French king. The Princess is a high spirited and witty lady, a perfect match for the king, as it turns out. But before the match can be made, she, together with her ladies, chastises the young courtiers of Navarre for their rude behavior and for their absurd rejection of the laws of love.

Rosaline, Maria, and Katherine

These ladies attending the Princess playfully engage in the game of rejecting their suitors, and, with her, demand a waiting period of one year before they will allow Biron, Longaville, and Dumain to approach them again.

Don Adriano de Armado

Shakespeare describes him as a "fantastical Spaniard." Armado is the parody of a courtly lover; he vies with the "clown" Costard for the favors of the country girl Jaquenetta.

Moth

Don Armado's diminutive, sharp-tongued page.

Holofernes

The pedantical schoolmaster. He and his sidekick, the curate Nathaniel, make their appearance in Act IV. They provide a comic reflection of the sophisticated language in the play; their odd conversations are filled with pompous elocutions and convoluted attempts at wit. All of the secondary characters take part in a courtly performance at the end of the play, a mock-reflection of the "masque" engaged in by the main characters.

Costard

He is Don Armado's rival for the country wench Jaquenetta.

Dull

The country constable whose name describes his facility with language and therefore places him in sharp contrast with the genteel and witty central characters.

SUMMARIES AND COMMENTARIES

ACT I – SCENE 1

Summary

As the play opens, the King of Navarre declares to his attendant lords, Longaville, Dumain, and Biron, that

> Navarre shall be the wonder of the world;
> Our court shall be a little Academe,
> Still and contemplative in living art [the art of living].
> (12-14)

He reminds his fellows that they have sworn to live in the court for three years as celibate scholars. Longaville and Dumain quickly consent to sign the king's statutes, the former declaring that it should be easy enough to comply for " 'tis but a three years' fast," and the latter emphatically asserting that from henceforth he is dead "to love, to wealth, to pomp." Biron, however, finds it difficult to be enthusiastic:

> O, these are barren tasks, too hard to keep,
> Not to see ladies, study, fast, not sleep!
>
> (47-48)

"I only swore to study with your grace," Biron objects, commencing the play's first witty exchange of dialogue. If the purpose of study is to learn things which otherwise he should not know, Biron argues, then it is only natural that a person should seek just those areas of knowledge which the statutes preclude him from. His gist is based in common sense:

> Why, all delights are vain, but that most vain
> Which, with pain purchased, doth inherit pain:
> As, painfully to pore upon a book,
> To seek the light of truth, while truth the while
> Doth falsely blind the eyesight of his look.
>
> (72-76)

Navarre detects an irony in this resistance to study and "continual plodding," for Biron's rational process itself owes its force to the books he decries; "How well he's read, to reason against reading!" Dumain and Longaville quickly chime in, forcing Biron to submit to the pressure: "I'll keep what I have swore." He requests one last perusal of the written decree to which he is to sign his name, and the king applauds him: "How well this yielding rescues thee from shame!"

Reading the articles aloud, Biron is surprised at the severity of the first (that any woman who comes within a mile of the court shall have her tongue removed), and he comments that it will be impossible for the king to observe the letter of the second (that any man seen talking to a woman shall endure public shame). The King of France's daughter, it seems, is scheduled to visit the court on state business. Embarrassed, Navarre tells the courtiers they will have to "dispense with this decree." Biron furthermore predicts the futility of Navarre's whole idea:

> Necessity will make us all forsworn
> Three thousand times within this three years' space:
> For every man with his affects [passions] is born,
> Not by might mastered, but by special grace.
>
> (150-53)

The skeptical Biron does finally sign his name to the document, however, asking his lord if there might not be some amusement for them, some "quick recreation" before their three-year dedication gets under way. A Spanish courtier by the name of Armado will serve for entertainment, Navarre promises:

> A man in all the world's new fashion planted,
> That hath a mint of phrases in his brain. . . .
>
> (165-66)

The constable (Dull) and a country bumpkin (Costard), who has been detained for consorting with a woman, round out the set of characters in the first scene. The King reads from an absurdly over-written letter by Armado in which Costard's "crime" is delineated:

King:	"There did I see that low-spirited swain, that base minnow of thy mirth—"
Costard:	Me?
King:	"That unlettered small-knowing soul—"
Costard:	Me?
King:	"That shallow vassal—"
Costard:	Still me!
King:	Which, as I remember, hight [is called] Costard—"
Costard:	O me!

                                                            (251-59)

Costard admits being acquainted with the proclamation forbidding traffic with women, though he has heard "little of the marking of it." Biron is sure that the oaths and laws will "prove an idle scorn."

Commentary

Shakespeare begins this ebullient youthful comedy by opposing two worlds with which young people are well-acquainted—that of school tasks and study on the one hand and, on the other, that of physical enjoyment and, in particular, the delights of the opposite sex. From the beginning, it seems clear that Navarre's scheme to establish a "wonder of the world" by instituting an ascetic academic community in his court is doomed to failure. Scarcely moments after Biron has groaned at the prospect of not seeing women, at being restricted to one meal each day, being forced to fast completely one day in seven, and to restrict himself to a mere three hours sleep per night, it turns out that Navarre himself cannot meet *all* the conditions he has set down. From the start, we know Navarre's plan is crackbrained; the fun will be in watching how it crumbles before the insatiable tugs of human passion, or "affections" to use Shakespeare's word. When Biron says, "I swore [to observe the rules] in jest," we can fully understand what he means; as for the others, their willingness to abjure "the world's delights" strikes a false chord.

Much of the delight in *Love's Labour's Lost* for a reader or theatergoer is in the pleasant artifice of the language, as sprightly as the characters who utter it. An example from the first scene sets the tone. The exchange has to do with Biron's logic in resisting Navarre's plan:

King:	How well he's read, to reason against reading!
Dumain:	Proceeded [educated] well, to stop all good proceeding!
Longaville:	He weeds the corn, and still lets grow the weeding.
Biron:	The spring is near, when green geese are a-breeding.
Dumain:	How follows that?
Biron:	Fit in his place and time.
Dumain:	In reason nothing.
Biron:	Something then in rhyme.

(94-101)

Biron short-circuits the teasing banter of his mates with a non sequitur which, he asserts, has its justification in the fact that it rhymes: reading, proceeding, weeding, a-breeding. One can almost hear the horselaughs and raspberries his friends greet that one with. The high spirits are what Shakespeare emphasizes here, and he entertains his audience with the end rhymes, silly as they are, here and throughout the play. Elsewhere, he will use the rhyme for different effects.

Note the conventional separation of character and delineation of mood through variety of language in this scene. Whereas the young nobles speak verse, the entry of the "low" characters, Dull and

Costard, is accompanied by a shift to prose. Costard's concluding lament, complete with a clanging malapropism, is typical:

> I suffer for the truth, sir, for true it is I was
> taken with Jaquenetta, and Jaquenetta is a
> true girl. And therefore welcome the sour cup
> of prosperity! Affliction may one day smile
> again, and till then sit thee down, sorrow!
>
> (313-17)

A further contrast of language and character comes through in scene one in the form of the letter from the caricature Spaniard, Armado. Armado is as overly florid in speech as Dull is dull. Shakespeare is drawing lines in *Love's Labour's Lost* between moderation and extremes, with the norm being defined in terms of the Elizabethan notion of a well-bred gentleman. The academic absurdities of Navarre, it turns out, are just as silly as the self-indulgent rhetoric of Armado: too much learning, too much (false) passion are to give way in the comedy to sensible middle courses of behavior.

Many scholars believe that Shakespeare wrote *Love's Labour's Lost* as a topical satire aimed at contemporary court fashions and behavior, and that he may even be referring to actual people from Elizabeth's court in specific characters (*e.g.*, Sir Walter Raleigh). This may be true and it is enlightening to know something of the particulars of literary, social, and intellectual fashions at the time (the fascination with Platonic theories of love, the delight in extravagant and often convoluted language, etc.), yet the play can be read or, with judicious cutting, be played on stage without the need for mountains of footnotes.

ACT I – SCENE 2

Summary

The pompous Spanish military man, Don Armado, engages his page, Moth, in conversation about his (the Don's) emotional quandary. He loves the "country girl" Jaquenetta, and at the start of the scene, he is out of sorts: "Boy, what sign is it when a man of great spirit grows melancholy?" The page steadily twits his dull-witted master, while apparently entertaining him with clever turns of phrase. As Armado puts it, he is "quick in answers." One example of an extended quibble they engage in has to do with the number three, as Armado says, "I have promised to study three years with the Duke."

Moth:	Then I am sure you know how much of the gross sum of deuce-ace amounts to.
Armado:	It doth amount to one more than two.
Moth:	Which the base vulgar do call three.
Armado:	True.
Moth:	Why, sir, is this such a piece of study? Now here is three studied ere ye'll thrice wink; and how easy it is to put 'years' to the word 'three,' and study three years in two words, the dancing horse will tell you.
Armado:	A most fine figure [of speech].
Moth:	[aside] To prove you a cipher.

(47-58)

The object of Armado's affections soon enters, together with Costard and Dull, and she treats him little better than his page.

Armado:	I will visit thee at the lodge.
Jaquenetta:	That's hereby.
Armado:	I know where it is situate.
Jaquenetta:	Lord, how wise you are!
Armado:	I will tell thee wonders.
Jaquenetta:	With that face?

(140-45)

Dull tells Armado that it is the duke's pleasure that he should be responsible for meting out Costard's punishment of three days' fast per week. The scene ends with a grotesque soliloquy in which Armado declares the extent of his love for Jaquenetta.

Commentary

Armado is ugly; "with that face," Jaquenetta exclaims, looking at him, and possibly he is also corpulent, as were many of the bragging

Spanish soldier types in the *commedia dell'arte*, the professional Italian touring troupes with which Shakespeare was surely acquainted. Armado is undoubtedly an affected ass. His page, taking the hint from his name, which suggests a "mote" or speck, is quite the opposite, probably diminutive and quick in body as well as mind. This is a comedy pair, at the heart of the subplot, doing virtually everything the characters from the "high" social stratum are capable of in exaggerated and absurd manner. The tedious word games with which Moth entertains Armado are difficult to sustain even for the servant, hence the frequent asides. And the spectacle of Armado as a "gentleman lover," here enraptured by a country wench, acts as a foil to the sets of lovers in the main plot.

Shakespeare has written the part of Armado in the vein of a *commedia* Braggart, and of course in the age of the Spanish Armada (the character's name even echoes this) the English audience would especially enjoy the lampoon of their archrival nation. Armado's speech calls for extravagance and improvisation, as would be the case in a *commedia dell'arte* performance. It also parodies the elaborate word displays of Shakespeare's educated contemporaries:

> Armado: I do affect the very ground (which is base) where her shoe (which is basest) doth tread. I shall be forsworn (which is a great argument of falsehood) if I love. And how can that be true love which is falsely attempted? Love is a familiar [spirit]; Love is a devil. There is no evil angel but Love.
>
> (172-77)

This goes on for thirteen more lines, proceeding by a loose association of ideas, imprinting on the audience's mind the depths of Armado's tediousness.

ACT II – SCENE 1

Summary

A formal grouping of the Princess of France with three attendant lords and three ladies takes the stage. The nobleman Boyet sings the Princess's praises ("Yourself held precious in the world's esteem"), while he urges her to represent her father's interest well to "Matchless Navarre." The King of France still owes 100,000 crowns to Navarre in repayment for money spent by the latter's father in the wars. As equity for the loan, Navarre keeps one part of Aquitaine. He later explains:

> If then the King your father will restore
> But that one half which is unsatisfied,
> We will give up our right in Aquitaine,
> And hold fair friendship with his majesty.
>
> (139-42)

But before Navarre arrives on the scene, we are given an insight into the Princess's spirited character. She bids Boyet to forego his flattery:

> Good Lord Boyet, my beauty, though but mean,
> Needs not the painted flourish of your praise.
> Beauty is bought by judgment of the eye,
> Not utt'red by base sale of chapmen's tongues.
>
> (13-16)

She knows of Navarre's "three year vow," and therefore she bids Boyet to intercede for her. At Boyet's exit, the Princess turns to her ladies and asks sarcastically about Navarre's companions.

> Who are the votaries [fellow vow-takers], my loving lords,
> That are vow-fellows with this virtuous duke?
>
> (37-38)

In turn, the women answer, each naming the nobleman who struck her eye when last they met: Maria remembers Longaville, "a man of sovereign parts" who also has "too blunt a will"; Katherine mentions Dumain, "a well-accomplished youth"; and Rosaline says that when Biron speaks, "younger hearings are quite ravished." The Princess is astonished: "God bless my ladies! Are they all in love?"

Boyet interrupts the talk by returning to announce that Navarre "means to lodge you in the field" rather than break his vow. The ladies don masks as Navarre, Biron, Dumain, and Longaville enter. The Princess's sharp tongue takes Navarre by surprise:

> King: Fair Princess, welcome to the court of Navarre.
> Princess: "Fair" I give you back again; and "welcome" I have not yet. The roof of this court is too high to be yours, and welcome to the wide fields too base to be mine.
>
> (90-94)

Biron and Rosaline echo the playfully hostile exchange of their superiors:

> Biron: What time o' day?
> Rosaline: The hour that fools should ask.
> Biron: Now fair befall your mask.
> Rosaline: Fair fall the face it covers!
> Biron: And send you many lovers!
> Rosaline: Amen, so you be none.
> Biron: Nay, then will I be gone.
>
> (122-28)

Dumain asks Boyet about Katherine ("heir of Alencon") and Longaville about Maria ("heir of Falconbridge") before they depart. The Princess interrupts a testy exchange between Katherine and Boyet to admonish them: "This civil war of wits were much better used/On Navarre and his book-men, for here 'tis abused." The scene draws to a close with sixteen lines of rhymed couplets in which Boyet interprets Navarre's loving looks—"all eyes saw his eyes enchanted with gazes"—as proof that the princess will most likely be able to recover Aquitaine for the price of a kiss.

Commentary

Shakespeare draws the lines for his love comedy with perfect symmetry in this scene. The battle of the sexes will be a battle of wits, matching the Princess and her three ladies against Navarre and his three lords. At this juncture, Boyet functions as a go-between and commentator. Both the Princess and Rosaline speak with the verve and tough beauty of Shakespeare's heroines in such more mature plays as *As You Like It* and *Twelfth Night*. That the Princess disarms Navarre in this scene is more than possible, if Boyet can be believed. Part of the fun in the comedy derives from showing the mastermind of the "three years' abstinence" idea as falling in love at first sight. On stage, with a good actor, this could be made clear easily enough and would not need be broadcast to the audience. Navarre's broken lines when speaking to the Princess ("Hear me, dear lady—I have sworn an oath") indicate some hesitation in his speech. And the Princess describes herself as "too sudden-bold," as if she noticed him being schoolboyish in his dealing with her. The King does become quite efficient when talking business (the loan, Acquitaine, etc.), but one wonders if there is more than mere formality in his words when he tells her upon parting that "you shall deem yourself lodged in my heart." Any attraction Navarre does feel, of course, he would also be desperate to hide from his fellow "votaries." It is perfectly obvious that each of them, in turn, is already infatuated with his female counterpart, and vice-versa. From this point on, it appears that "love's labour" will not really be "lost."

Notice the style of language in this scene. Boyet's request at the start of the scene that the Princess show herself to the best possible advantage is typically elegant:

> Be now as prodigal of all dear grace,
> As Nature was in making graces dear
> When she did starve the general world beside
> And prodigally gave them all to you.
>
> (9-12)

There does come a point, however, at which the rhyme used in the scene grows tedious. Even if Shakespeare meant thereby to make a comment on the character speaking, as in the following, there remains a problem for modern audiences. Boyet finishes his speech on Navarre's self-betraying looks thus:

> His face's own margent did quote such amazes
> That all eyes saw his eyes enchanted with gazes.
> I'll give you Aquitaine, and all that is his,
> And you give him for my sake but one loving kiss.
>
> (246-49)

The Princess dismisses him: "Come to our pavilion. Boyet is disposed."

ACT III – SCENE 1

Summary

Moth sings a "sweet air" for Armado, then gives him advice on how to secure his love—through song, dance, face-pulling, and rhetorical devices. The conversation meanders here and there at the whim of the clever Moth, causing Armado to remark on his "sweet smoke of rhetoric." Moth fetches Costard at his master's behest, and the nonsensical language games now include the newcomer. Even Costard can see that Moth is making a fool of his master, "The boy hath sold him a bargain, a goose."

> *Moth:*   Now will I begin your moral, and do you follow
> with my l'envoy.
> > The fox, the ape, and the humblebee
> > Were still at odds, being but three.
>
> *Armado:* Until the goose came out of door,
> Staying the odds by adding four.
>
> *Moth:*   A good l'envoy, ending in the goose.
>
> > > (94-100)

Armado, of course, is the "goose" who ends the ditty.

Costard is twice bid to become a postman, to deliver a love letter from Armado to Jaquenetta (for which he is paid "remuneration"), and to deliver a note from Biron to Rosaline (for this, he gets a "guerdon" [reward]). Making his exit, he exclaims:

> Gardon, O sweet gardon! Better than remuneration—
> a 'levenpence farthing better. Most sweet gardon!
> I will do it sir, in print [with care]. Gardon!
> Remuneration!
>
> > > (171-74)

To cap the scene, Shakespeare radically shifts to a loftier style in the person of Biron, who delivers a thirty-three-line soliloquy expressing the quandary in which he finds himself. It begins: "O, and I, forsooth, in love!"

Commentary

The broad contrasts which characterize the structure of *Love's Labour's Lost* are apparent at the beginning and the end of this scene. Armado is a braggart and a fool in love, a caricature of the transformations which can take place when a man is prey to his passions. The first moments of the scene are broadly comical, commencing as Moth sings a sweet tune to suit the master's mood (compare the opening of *Twelfth Night*: "If music be the food of love, play on."), then going on to include a demonstration by Moth of the ways to woo a woman. Though there are no stage directions, it seems likely that Moth would at least illustrate (and perhaps coax Armado into performing) some of the physical techniques he describes: "No, my complete master; but to jig off a tune at the tongue's end, canary to it with your feet, humour it with turning up your eyelids. . . ." The same comical teaching takes place in a parallel scene with Toby Belch, Maria, and Andrew Aguecheek in *Twelfth Night* (I, 3).

At the other end of the spectrum, and the scene, is the nobleman Biron, also in love, wrestling with his feelings in a far more dignified manner. Love is transforming him as well:

> I, that have been love's whip,
> A very beadle to a humorous sigh,
> A critic, nay, a night-watch constable. . . .
> And I to be a corporal of his [Cupid's] field,
> And wear his colours like a tumbler's hoop!
> What? I love? I sue? I seek a wife!

> (173-79)

But there is a rightness in this change, it turns out, for the world of Shakespeare's happy comedy demands the triumph of love over artificial barriers.

The two love letters to be delivered by the utter, literal fool, Costard, are bound to be mixed up. Shakespeare stirs the action and excites the audience's expectation by this device. Notice, however, how relatively unimportant this sort of detail is in *Love's Labour's Lost* by comparison to *The Comedy of Errors*. The life of the later comedy is less in its plot than in its language, and to a certain extent, its character.

ACT IV – SCENE 1

Summary

The Princess and her retinue are in an open park preparing for a hunt. "But come, the bow!" she calls, after seeing a rider in the distance and asking:

> Was that the King, that spurred his horse so hard
> Against the steep uprising of the hill?
>
> (1-2)

She engages the Forester in conversation, displaying her intellectual superiority with puns and clever turns of phrase before rewarding him with money. After a lengthy speech on the pursuit of fame, she says,

> And, out of question, so it is sometimes,
> Glory grows guilty of detested crimes,
> When, for fame's sake, for praise, an outward part,
> We bend to that the working of the heart;
> As I for praise alone now seek to spill
> The poor deer's blood that my heart means no ill.
>
> (30-35)

and the Princess then turns her attention to Costard, who has just entered with a letter which, he says, is addressed from Monsieur Biron to Lady Rosaline. "O, thy letter, thy letter! He's a good friend of mine," she exclaims boldly, requesting Boyet to read the missive at once. The letter is, in fact, from Armado to Jaquenetta, written in the most bizarre meandering style:

> Shall I command thy love? I may. Shall I enforce thy love? I could. Shall I entreat thy love? I will. What shall thou exchange for rags? Robes. For tittles? Titles. For thyself? Me. Thus, expecting thy reply, I propose my lips on thy foot, my eyes on thy picture, and my heart on thy every part.
>
> (81-86)

"What plume of feathers is that indited [wrote] this letter?" asks the Princess. She tells Costard that he has misdelivered the letter, then exits with all but Boyet, Maria, Rosaline, and Costard. Boyet teases Rosaline, who responds in sharp form. It is Maria's turn next to banter with Boyet over the affair. As their speech grows more and more bawdy, Costard chimes in with an obviously obscene remark, causing Maria to say, "Come, come, you talk greasily." Costard has enjoyed the chatter immensely, convinced that he and the ladies have "put him [Armado, and perhaps Boyet] down." He loves the "most sweet jests, most incony [excellent] vulgar wit."

Commentary

The display of wit is a chief resource of the characters in this play. To start the scene, the Princess aims her wit at an easy target, a Forester assisting her on the hunt. When he tells her that she is to have the "fairest shoot," she coyly takes it to mean that she is the fairest one who will shoot. The Princess and her retinue surely enjoy the Forester's befuddlement: "Pardon me, madam, for I meant not so." These pleasantries at the expense of a member of a lower class of society were quite normal in Shakespeare's day, as reflected in his comedies. To end the scene, another "low" character, the rustic (or "clown," as Shakespeare refers to him) Costard joins the verbal games with his betters. Boyet's suggestive language, "And if my hand be out, then belike your hand is in," prompts Costard's "Then will she get the upshoot by cleaving the pin." "Pin" refers to the male sex organ, and the talk merits a rebuke from Maria. Shakespeare contrasts the refinement of the Princess's airy allusions to Cupid and his bow at the front of the scene, to the sexual reality of romantic love here at the end. In his better plays, he manages to intermingle these two in a more interesting manner.

The Princess's musings on the subjects of "fame" and "glory," quoted in the summary above, sound a central note of the play. Her philosophical bent from the first time we met her was such that she played down the importance of external beauty, or external virtues of any kind. All the while she is speaking, remember, and throughout the scene she has a hunting bow in hand (Cupid's symbol). The implicit metaphor of the bow as a means of subduing game, if not killing it, as it relates to the battle between love's demands (Cupid's) and man's or woman's resistance to those demands, can be extended to the "battle" between the sexes. Boyet teases the Princess, saying that women try to "lord it over" their lords "for praise's sake," and she responds haughtily:

> Only for praise, and praise we may afford
> To any lady that subdues a lord.

(39-40)

When Costard asks for "the head lady," the Princess says that she is the "thickest and tallest." Costard then says that it must be *she*, for she is the "thickest." It is unlikely that he would insult her outright— "thick" can normally mean "corpulent" or "stupid," or both. It is, of course, possible that some of the Princess's insistence on the irrelevance of external shape is prompted by her own slightly large frame. She *does* respond to Costard's words in a huff: "What's your will, sir? What's your will?"

The long nonsense letter from Armado, read aloud by Boyet, allows the actor ample opportunity to lampoon the hyperbolic style of the braggart Spaniard, but in the context of the comedy as a whole, it allows for a mockery (including self-mockery) of all the courtly lovers in danger of making fools of themselves in pursuit of their partners.

ACT IV – SCENE 2

Summary

Together with Dull, two new characters—Holofernes the pedant and Nathaniel—enter the hunting park. The three engage in a very odd conversation, larded with pompous elocutions, misunderstandings, and convoluted stabs at wit. Typically, Holofernes holds forth on the subject of the deer which the Princess has just killed:

> The deer was, as you know, *sanguis*, in blood; ripe as the pomewater, who now hangeth like a jewel in the ear of *caelo*, the sky, the welkin, the heaven; and anon falleth like a crab on the face of *terra*, the soil, the land, the earth.

(3-7)

Holofernes, this dubious teacher of English youth, dominates the talk: "if their sons be ingenious, they shall want no instruction; if their daughters be capable, I will put it to them." As he concludes one long speech with the Latin expression "*Vir sapit qui pauca loquitur*" (he who speaks little is wise), a "soul feminine" approaches: Jaquenetta.

She greets the parson Holofernes and asks him to read a letter for her. It is the message from Biron to Rosaline, in the form of a sonnet which Nathaniel reads out to the others: "If love make me forsworn, how shall I swear to love?" Holofernes criticizes the reading ("You find not the apostrophas, and so miss the accent") and further offers to appraise the poem itself for Nathaniel later at dinner. "I will prove those verses to be very unlearned," he promises, "neither savoring of poetry, wit, nor invention."

Commentary

For Holofernes, the rule of speech is never to avoid an opportunity for affectation or for display of pedantry. In his hierarchy of characters, Shakespeare has created them according to their facility with words; Holofernes, thus, is a caricature of the master of language. He is in the tradition of the Dottore character from the Italian *commedia dell'arte* just as Armado is in the tradition of the *commedia* braggart and Spaniard. "O thou monster ignorance," exclaims Holofernes, though his abuse of learning is infinitely sillier than the homespun ignorance of other characters. The conversation between Nathaniel, Dull, and the schoolmaster is highly entertaining:

Dull: You two are book-men. Can you tell me by your wit

What was a month old at Cain's birth, that's not five weeks old as yet?

Holofernes: Dictynna, goodman Dull. Dictynna, goodman Dull.

Dull: What is Dictynna?

Nathaniel: A title to Phoebe, to Luna, to the moon.

Holofernes: The moon was a month old when Adam was no more.

And raught [reached] not to five weeks when he came to fivescore.

Th' allusion holds in the exchange.

Dull:	'Tis true indeed; the collusion holds in the exchange.
Holofernes:	God comfort thy capacity! I say th' allusion holds in the exchange.
Dull:	And I say the pollusion holds in the exchange, for the moon is never but a month old; and I say beside that, 'twas a pricket that the Princess killed.

(35-47)

Dull opens the gambit with a typical Elizabethan delight in riddles, whereupon the schoolmaster counters with pedantry, and the whole exchange dissolves into a stuttering of misunderstandings. The pleasure in this part of the scene resides purely in the comic language and general satire. Holofernes's delivery of his "extemporal epitaph" on the death of the deer calls for a virtuoso turn of mock elocution: "The preyful princess pierced and pricked a pretty pleasing pricket. . . ." His protégé Nathaniel applauds: "a rare talent!"

Compared to Holofernes's fractured language, of course, the poem which Biron has written to Rosaline is elegant and delightfully sophistic. He argues in the poem that his "wrong" (breaking the academic vow) should be divinely condoned.

The eye Jove's lightning bears, thy voice his dreadful thunder,
Which, not to anger bent, is music and sweet fire.
Celestial as thou art, O, pardon love this wrong,
That sings heaven's praise with such an earthly tongue!

(119-22)

ACT IV – SCENE 3

Summary

Biron reads from a soul-searching composition: "I will not love; if I do, hang me! I'faith, I will not. O but her eye! . . . By heaven, I do love, and it hath taught me to rhyme and to be melancholy. . . ." When the King enters, a sheet of paper in his hand, Biron ducks out of sight and listens with pleasure as his monarch reads from a sonnet he has written:

> O queen of queens, how far dost thou excel
> No thought can think, nor tongue of mortal tell!
>
> (40-41)

The comedy builds rapidly with Longaville entering, the King duck-ing aside, then Dumain coming onto the scene and forcing Longaville into hiding. Each in turn reads from his own lyrical expression of love, unaware of the presence of the others. Then they are exposed in turn, with Biron the last to emerge to accuse the King of hypocrisy for upbraiding Dumain and Longaville, who have broken their vows:

> Now step I forth to whip hypocrisy.
> Oh, good my liege, I pray thee, pardon me.
> Good heart, what grace hast thou thus to reprove
> These worms for loving, that art most in love?
>
> (151-54)

After this accusation, Biron also suffers the obligatory embarrass-ment, because Costard, bearing Biron's missive to Rosaline, has un-expectedly appeared. Jacquenetta asks that the letter be read, because "our parson [Holofernes] misdoubts it; 'twas treason, he said." Biron tries to wriggle free, but Dumain pieces together the shreds of paper which Biron has made of the letter.

> *Dumain:*   It is Biron's writing, and here is his name.
> *Biron:* [to Costard]:   Ah, you whoreson loggerhead, you were born to do me shame! Guilty, my lord, guilty. I confess, I confess.

Biron heartily calls for them all to recognize their folly:

> Sweet lords, sweet lovers, O, let us embrace!
> As true we are as flesh and blood can be.
> The sea will ebb and flow, heaven show his face;
> Young blood doth not obey an old decree.
>
> (214-17)

Joined by Dumain and Longaville, the King enters a genteel slanging match with Biron over the relative merits of their preferred women. At the King's request,

> But what of this? Are we not all in love? . . .
> Then leave this chat, and, good Biron, now prove
> Our loving lawful and our faith not torn,
>
> (282-84)

Biron rationalizes their unanimous (though independently arrived at) choice to countermand the vows of chastity:

> To fast, to study, and to see no woman—
> Flat treason 'gainst the kingly state of youth.
>
> (292-93)

The scene ends in jubilation as the King bids them all prepare some entertainment with which to woo their ladies. They all agree with Biron:

> In the afternoon
> We will with some strange pastime solace them,
> Such as the shortness of the time can shape;
> For revels, dances, masks, and merry hours
> Forerun fair Love, strewing her way with flowers.
>
> (376-80)

Commentary

Scene 3 is a classical piece of comedy. Each of the young men is exposed, while the audience enjoys the process of their mutual deceit leading up to the final moment. Following the conventions of Elizabethan staging, one must imagine each of the lovers hiding from the others while in full view of the audience. It is simply accepted dramatically that when they speak their "asides" to the audience, the main "onstage" character doesn't hear them. Biron is most likely tucked away in the tiring house (the rear wall) facade or placed in a practicab' 'age property tree ("like a demigod here sit I in the sky") while he looks down on the foolishness of his peers. The others are distributed about the stage.

Notice the style of each "love sonnet": the King's opens conventionally with the syrup of courtly love:

> So sweet a kiss the golden sun gives not
> To those fresh morning drops upon the rose,
> As thy eye-beams when their fresh rays have smote
> The night of dew that on my cheeks down flows.
>
> (26-29)

Then it "progresses" to lovers' melancholy:

> But do not love thyself—then thou will keep
> My tears for glasses [mirrors] and still make me weep.
>
> (38-39)

Longaville engages in sophistry, intellectually justifying his aberrance:

> A woman I forswore, but I will prove,
> Thou being a goddess, I forswore not thee.
>
> (64-65)

This remark elicits Biron's ironic judgment from "on high": "Pure, pure idolatry./God amend us, God amend!" It is ironic because Biron is a past-master at just this sort of intellectual conceit.

Dumain's attempt is the least accomplished, though his intent is the same as the others:

> On a day—alack the day!—
> Love, whose month is ever May,
> Spied a blossom passing fair
> Playing in the wanton air. . . .
> Do not call it sin in me,
> That I am forsworn for thee.
>
> (101-6)

His "private wish" is no sooner uttered than he discovers that it has been true all along:

> O, would the King, Biron, and Longaville
> Were lovers too!
>
> (123-24)

The greatest fall is amusingly reserved for the man whose position is most haughty. Biron lays it on thick when he berates his fellows:

> I that am honest, I that hold it sin
> To break the vow I am engaged in;
> I am betrayed by keeping company
> With men like you, men of inconstancy.
> When shall you see me write a thing in rhyme?
> Or groan for love?
>
> (177-82)

The tone of the scene is jolly, however, and the satire is not calculated to "draw blood," as was true for hypocrites attacked by Shakespeare's contemporary, Ben Jonson, or would be true in Moliere's great comedies of the seventeenth century. The four lovers playfully attack one another, boyishly teasing each other about the virtues of their ladies:

> Biron: Your mistresses dare never come in rain,
>   For fear their colours should be washed away.
> King: 'Twere good yours did; for, sir, to tell you plain,
>   I'll find a fairer face not washed today.
> Biron: I'll prove her fair or talk till doomsday here.
>   (270-74)

The seventy-line "justification" uttered by Biron at the end of the scene offers a special insight into Shakespeare's process of composing his early plays. In most editions of the play, this section beginning with "And where that you have vowed to study, lords" and concluding with "Do we not likewise see our learning there?" will be bracketed, or set apart as redundant. The fact is, these lines are essentially no different from the following ones, indicating that Shakespeare re-cast the thoughts into sharper poetical language. His printer probably overlooked the deletion and set both sections of the speech. Compare the two passages for effectiveness.

Biron sings the praises of love as a teacher and a spur to intellectual and creative energy. He claims that it gives "to every power a double power," compared to "slow arts" (mere book-learning) which "scarce show a harvest of their heavy toil." His peroration deservedly earns the accolade of his King.

> Then fools you were these women to forswear,
> Or, keeping what is sworn, you will prove fools.
> For wisdom's sake, a word that all men love,
> Or for love's sake, a word that loves all men,
> Or for men's sake, the authors of these women,
> Or women's sake, by whom we men are men—
> Let us once lose our oaths to find ourselves,
> Or else we lose ourselves to keep our oaths.
>
> (355-62)

Fittingly, the King declares a new allegiance to usher the men to follow the urgings of their passion and to draw the scene to a close:

> Saint Cupid then! And, soldiers, to the field!
>
> (366)

ACT V—SCENE 1

Summary

Don Armado beseeches Holofernes to help him prepare "some delightful ostentation, or show, or pageant, or antic, or firework" to entertain the Princess, as the King desires. Holofernes proposes "The Nine Worthies," in which he himself will play three of the parts, and the rest of the sub-plot figures (Costard, Dull, Moth, and Armado) will fill in the others.

Commentary

The heart of the comedy in this scene is the meeting between the master of effusive digression, Armado, with the master of pedantic blabber, Holofernes. Both are mocked by the diminutive Moth and are observed in awe by "goodman" Dull, who speaks no word until the end of the scene, and then as he says, "Nor understood none neither." *Love's Labour's Lost* was certainly played before an educated Elizabethan audience, if not expressly commissioned by the highly cultured nobility. Such an audience would undoubtedly have enjoyed the lampoon of pretentious academics offered here. (Some critics even claim that this early play reveals Shakespeare's recent experiences as a rural schoolmaster, before he dedicated himself to the stage). The Latin quotations and extended linguistic quibbles would, for the most part, be lost on a modern audience, though with some cutting the sense of the comedy can remain intact. Among the secondary characters, Moth's wit is sharpest: "They have been at a great feast of languages," he tells Costard, "and stol'n the scraps."

Compounding Holofernes's pretentiousness is his hypocrisy. After privately disparaging Don Armado's habit of drawing "out the thread of his verbosity finer than the staple [fibre] of his argument" at the beginning of the scene, he later unctuously compliments Armado to his face (possibly with a sarcastic wink to Nathaniel) on his skillful embroidery of language:

> *Armado:* Sir, it is the King's most sweet pleasure and affection to congratulate the Princess at her pavilion in the posteriors [hindquarters] of this day, which the rude multitude call the afternoon.
>
> *Holofernes:* The posterior of the day, most generous sir, is liable, congruent, and measurable for the afternoon. The word is well culled, chose, sweet and apt, I do assure you, sir, I do assure.
>
> (92-99)

This scene naturally contrasts to the previous one, in which the well-bred characters engaged in their own language games and then were mildly chided for hypocrisy. Remember that Shakespeare expected these scenes to flow from one to the other without act or scene divisions as such, thus sharpening the contrast.

ACT V – SCENE 2

Summary

The Princess, Katherine, Rosaline, and Maria discuss the way they have been flattered and showered with gifts by the King and his court.

The Princess mockingly refers to Navarre's poetry – "as much love in a rhyme/As would be crammed up in a sheet of paper" – and each of the others likewise complains about the excessive verbiage they have been assailed with: "The letter is too long by half a mile." The women comment on the ways of Cupid, deciding it is best to retain "a light heart" in love lest they suffer the fate of Katherine's sister:

> He [Cupid] made her melancholy, sad, and heavy;
> And so she died.
>
> (14-15)

All four wish they could "punish" these courtiers – "wits turned fool" – for their excesses, for not the least one imagines his silliness in vowing to abjure love at the outset of the play. "How I would make him [Biron] fawn, and beg, and seek. . . ." says Rosaline.

Boyet comes onto the stage with a burst of energy, beside himself with laughter at what he has overheard nearby in the park. The King and his entourage are on their way, elegantly costumed as Russians, preparing to woo the ladies. He observed them planning the courtly masque:

> With that, they all did tumble on the ground
> With such a zealous laughter, so profound,
> That in this spleen [passion] ridiculous appears,
> To check their folly, passion's solemn tears.
>
> (115-18)

On the spur of the moment, the Princess decides that they should foil the lords in their "mocking merriment" by donning masks to confuse the individual wooers as to whom they are rightly to pursue. "Should we dance?" she is asked.

> No, to the death, we will not move a foot,
> Nor to their penned speech render we no grace,
> But while 'tis spoke each turn away her face.
>
> (146-48)

Trumpet fanfare signals the arrival of the disguised courtiers, preceded by Moth, who tries to deliver a formal introductory speech.

He responds to the ladies' calculated rudeness by making impromptu changes in his delivery, much to Biron's consternation.

> *Moth:* "A holy parcel of the fairest dames,
> [The Ladies turn their backs to him.]
> That ever turned their – backs – to mortal views!"
> *Biron:* "Their eyes," villain, "their eyes!"
>
> (160-62)

As each of the men approaches a lady, he is met with the normal coquettish resistance, but none of them knows that they have been steered to the wrong ladies. Typical of the exchange is the following exchange between the King and Rosaline (whom he takes to be the Princess):

> *Rosaline:* We will not dance.
> *King:* Why take we hands then?
> *Rosaline:* Only to part friends.
> Curtsy, sweet hearts. And so the measure ends.
> *King:* More measure of this measure. Be not nice.
> *Rosaline:* We can afford no more at such a price.
> *King:* Price you yourselves. What buys your company?
> *Rosaline:* Your absence only.
>
> (218-25)

Biron and the Princess, Dumain and Maria, and Longaville and Katherine enact similar scenes, as each couple retires to speak further in private. Boyet enjoys the spectacle:

> The tongues of mocking wenches are as keen
> As is the razor's edge invisible. . . .
>
> (256-57)

He advises the ladies, once the "masquers" have departed, to continue the sport by blowing "like sweet roses in this summer air" when the men return without their costumes. Rosaline picks up the idea, enthusiastically adding:

58

> Let's mock them still, as well known as disguised.
> Let us complain to them what fools were here,
> Disguised like Muscovites in shapeless gear. . . .
>
> (301-3)

When Boyet acts as the go-between for the ladies to the King, the gentlemen eye him with contempt. He is the one nobleman privy to the ladies' chamber. Biron vents his frustration in Shakespeare's sharpest language:

> 'A [he: Boyet] can carve too, and lisp. Why this is he
> That kissed his hand away in courtesy.
> This is the ape of form [decorum], Monsieur the Nice
>   [exquisite],
> That, when he plays at tables, chides the dice
> In honorable terms. . . .
> The stairs, as he treads on them, kiss his feet.
>
> (323-30)

With the return of Boyet and the ladies, the "comedy of errors" is exposed, but not before the Princess squeezes her last moments of pleasure from the situation. When the King bids her to follow him to court, she displays false concern for his "sacred vow":

> This field shall hold me, and so hold your vow.
> Nor God nor I delights in perjured men.
>
> (345-46)

Rosaline adds her playful venom by discrediting the "Russian" visitors as boors:

> . . . in that hour, my lord,
> They did not bless us with one happy word.
>
> (369-70)

The ultimate exposure of their folly causes Biron to swear off fancy phrases for plain speech in declaring his love:

> Taffeta phrases, silken terms precise,
> Three-piled hyperboles, spruce affectation,

Figures pedantical — these summer flies
Have blown me full of maggot ostentation.
I do forswear them.

(406-10)

Each of the gentlemen realizes that he "wooed but the sign" of the lady whom he loved, and so ends this part of the scene.

Costard enters to announce the imminent arrival of the next entertainment, arranged by Armado and Holofernes. Though the King fears for his reputation, both Biron and the Princess insist that the performance take place:

Princess:
Nay, my good lord, let me o'errule you now.
That sport best pleases that doth least know how,
Where zeal strives to content, and the contents
Dies in the zeal of that which it presents.

(516-19)

Armado is to play Hector of Troy; Costard, Pompey the Great; Nathaniel, Alexander the Great; Moth, Hercules; and Holofernes, Judas Maccabaeus. Each of the performers speaks his piece and suffers the mocking interruptions of the audience. The gentlemen enjoy their heckling immensely, happy to transfer their own humiliation onto others. Biron, in passing, even grows fond of Boyet: "Well said, old mocker. I must needs be friends with thee." Holofernes plays his part true to pedantic form, first rationalizing away the casting of tiny Moth as the giant Hercules:

Great Hercules is presented by this imp,
Whose club killed Cerberus, that three-headed *canus* [dog];
And when he was a babe, a child, a shrimp,
Thus did he strangle serpents in his *manus* [hand].

(392-95)

When all the nobles descend on him with wisecracks, he skulks off sullenly — "This is not generous, not gentle, not humble" — and evokes the Princess's pity: "Alas, poor Maccabaeus, how hath he been baited!"

The play threatens to break down when Costard, apparently urged on by Biron, accuses Armado the warrior (Hector) that he has got Jaquenetta pregnant. The braggart backs down from a fight: "I will not combat in my shirt."

The mood changes abruptly when the messenger Mercade arrives to tell the Princess news of her father's death. Though he tries, the King cannot persuade her to remain with him. She vows to shut her "woeful self up in a mourning house" for one year, and she tells the King if he can preserve his love for her for one year in "a naked hermitage,/Remote from all the pleasures of the world," she will be his. Each of the other women proposes a similar waiting period to her suitor. Rosaline proposes a penance particularly suited to Biron, a man she calls "replete with mocks." He is to use his facility of speech to ease the pain of the sick:

> You shall this twelvemonth term from day to day
> Visit the speechless sick, and still converse
> With groaning wretches; and your task shall be
> With all the fierce endeavour of your wit
> To enforce the pained impotent to smile.
>
> (860-64)

He agrees to "jest a twelvemonth in a hospital," exclaiming for all four suitors:

> Our wooing doth not end like an old play;
> Jack hath not Jill.
>
> (884-85)

Shakespeare ends the play with an allegorical song performed by the figures of Winter and Spring, singing the song of the Owl and the Cuckoo, compiled by the "learned men" (as Armado informs us) in testament to life's vagaries, the "merry larks" of sunny days and the times when "blood is nipped."

Commentary

The courtly masque in Shakespeare's day was a combination of entertainment, allegorical story, and generous offering to genteel guests. It typically consisted of songs, dances, and elaborately costumed and designed pageants which were created by professional and amateur artists and in which the audience was meant to participate actively. Normally, at some point in the proceeding, the honored guests and their hosts would join in a dance with the entire costumed troupe. A feature of many masques was a grotesque counter- or anti-masque in which the songs and dances were bizarre, meant to represent negative qualities or evil influences in life, and which were calculated to show the featured "noble" masquers in a better light by contrast. Above all, spectacle dominated the performance.

In *Love's Labour's Lost*, Shakespeare plays on the different aspects of masques and masquing. When Biron says to the King that they should allow the "Nine Worthies" to be performed by the sub-plot characters, he notes that it will make their own efforts as "dancing Russians" seem less ridiculous. Holofernes's main performance is thus a kind of "anti-masque." When the gentlemen dress up as Muscovites and invite their ladies to dance, they are playing out the courtly wooing aspect of the masque, just as the ladies do when they don masks to deceive the men and protract the lovers' ritual. The spirit is one of abandon and hilarity, even though the ladies do their best to confound and embarrass the King and his courtiers. The elaborate plans to "play" with the men's feelings extend the idea of courtly love implicit in the masque tradition.

When Holofernes and his own troupe enter the scene we have a precursor of Shakespeare's "rude mechanicals" scene in *A Midsummer Night's Dream*, where the offering of *Pyramus and Thisbe* delights the nobility for its well-meaning incompetence. In *Love's Labour's Lost*, however, the satire is directed at the pomposity of the lead masquers, who have carried their classical learning to pretentious extremes.

Shakespeare broadly comments in this scene on the follies of men in love, as they are each, in turn, seen to have made fools of themselves, even to the point of taking the *wrong* women aside as objects of their love. In his plays, Shakespeare frequently ponders the frailty of the senses, the tricks which the passions can play. The desire "to be in love" led them, in part, to their silliest moments.

There is something arbitrary about the ending of the play. Love's labors are (temporarily) lost, once the hard reality of life is brought home to them all. The hilarity of the action abruptly stops with the news of the Princess's father's death, and Shakespeare rounds out the play with one of his most beautiful songs. The emotional tone of the ending – juxtaposing Winter and Spring and all they imply – relates to a philosophical acceptance of all aspects of life which one encounters in many of Shakespeare's plays, tragedies and comedies alike.

The Two Gentlemen of Verona

INTRODUCTION

Of the three plays in this volume, *Two Gentlemen of Verona* has the least merit. The plot is unlikely, even for a comedy; the motivations of the characters – Proteus, in particular – are so mercurial that an audience finds them hard to accept; and, finally, the ending seems absurdly unexpected, not so much through design, it seems, as through a desire to have done with the plot in a conventional and "satisfactorily" happy manner. Several Shakespearean critics take Shakespeare to task for his "uncertainty of metrical expression," but this matter seems to deal more with Shakespeare's poetics than with his sense of drama and comedy.

On the surface, the plot of this play seems promising, particularly at the beginning: a young man, Valentine, sets out in the world to seek his fortune and to find true love; meanwhile, his best friend, Proteus, remains at home to accomplish the same things. Very soon, however, this premise turns sour. The adventuresome young man falls immediately in love with a woman whom he can never wed because her father has promised her to another suitor. This is standard fare, and it could furnish both bittersweet romance and comedy – particularly if the lovers tried unsuccessfully to rendezvous a number of times. But the play begins seriously to wane as a comedy when Shakespeare metamorphoses the adventuresome young man's best friend, Proteus, into a villain. Originally, one supposes, Shakespeare was interested in the comic possibilities of the many things that might go awry when best friends fall in love with the same woman. This premise is sound. Shakespeare's play, however, fails to amuse us as soon as Proteus eagerly denounces his best friend, an act which results in Valentine's banishment – on threat of death. Moreover, Proteus was once deeply in love, we were led to believe, with Julia. However, when he sets eyes on the beautiful Silvia, he forgets about Julia entirely. Then, at the play's end, we are supposed to forgive this fraudulent cheat and be happy when he realizes that he really *does* love Julia, a young woman who has somehow managed to remain in love with him all this time.

The ready sacrifice of friendship, as well as the ready renunciation of love – in exchange for the *possibility* of wooing the beautiful Silvia is not the real stuff of light comedy. Faithlessness, unscrupulous behavior, and fraud make poor comic fare. Then, there is also the business of the banished Valentine being forced, as it were, to play Robin Hood to a band of ill-organized forest brigands.

The critic Quiller-Couch is absolutely convinced that Shakespeare was not responsible for writing the play's ending with a sudden double wedding in the offing. His arguments are convincing. Surely Shakespeare realized that he had created a villain in Proteus; after all, he renounces his best friend, Valentine, and his (allegedly) beloved Julia, and he tries to force Silvia to marry him. In contrast, oddly enough, Shakespeare was wholly successful in his Sonnets (written approximately the same time as this play) when he dealt with the vagaries and the complexities of love and friendship. But in the Sonnets, Shakespeare was being serious. His intent here is quite different; he wants to explore playfully both themes and present their comic aspects. To a large degree, Shakespeare fails; one laughs, but neither with gusto nor joy.

Perhaps the value of this play lies most in Shakespeare's first versions of characters who appear later in his more mature plays. Silvia's having to deal with a suitor whom she does not love and whom her father forces upon her foreshadows Juliet's distress; likewise, Valentine's banishment parallels Romeo's – but those two lovers were key characters in a tragedy. The comic Launce in *Two Gentlemen* prefigures Launcelot Gobbo (*The Merchant of Venice*), and Julia's disguising herself as a man in a dramatic convention that Shakespeare will later use with Portia, Nerissa, and Jessica (all in *The Merchant of Venice*), as well as with Rosalind (*As You Like It*) and Viola (*Twelfth Night*). *The Two Gentlemen of Verona* is, then, ultimately less of a successful comedy than it is an apprentice piece, containing the blueprints for later, more well-rounded characters. Most of all, the mastery which Shakespeare achieves in just a few years, when compared to his handling of this play, helps us to measure his genius.

BRIEF SYNOPSIS

The two "gentlemen" of the title are Proteus and Valentine, who are taking leave of one another as the play opens. Valentine travels to Milan, where he falls in love with Silvia, daughter of the Duke. Proteus, meanwhile, hunts after love and remains in Verona, pledged to faithfulness to his beloved Julia.

When Proteus travels to Milan, however, he too falls in love with Silvia and proceeds to undermine his friend by denouncing him to the Duke. Valentine is banished to the forest, where he joins a band of thieves. Proteus pursues Silvia more and more fervently, even to the point of threatening to take her violently. Julia arrives in Milan disguised as a page and joins herself to the unsuspecting Proteus, and the two of them "rescue" Silvia from the brigands to whom she had fled. At the moment when Proteus is about to attack Silvia, Valentine intercedes to save her. Astonishingly, Valentine is so overcome by his friend's anguish that he is even prepared to yield Silvia to Proteus. Julia swoons, and the page's true identity is revealed. Proteus now sees her as his true love, and the Duke arrives on stage to offer his daughter's hand to Valentine.

LIST OF CHARACTERS

Valentine

The first of the "gentlemen"; Valentine is early described by his friend Proteus as one who "after honor hunts" rather than after love. While abroad in Milan, Valentine succumbs to the charms of Silvia, the Duke's daughter, but before he is successfully united with her, he must suffer the indignity of betrayal by a friend and subsequent banishment to the forest, where he joins a band of robbers.

Proteus

The second "gentleman"; he transforms rapidly from a loyal friend and faithful lover into something of a villain when he too is struck by the charms of Silvia. He deserts Julia, plots to have Valentine banished, and is about to physically attack Silvia before he is interrupted at the last minute. His sudden remorse elicits Valentine's pity; all is forgiven, and Proteus is reunited with Julia.

Julia

In the early scenes of this play, Julia wrestles with her feelings for Proteus; within the context of youthful courtship, these feelings give way to later ones filled with the agony of rejection and the protracted spectacle of her beloved debasing himself out of love for another woman. Julia shows the spunk and charm of later Shakespearean heroines, especially in the scenes in which she disguises herself as a page (to Proteus) in the strange city of Milan.

Silvia

The Duke of Milan's high-spirited daughter; she is sought after by a number of eligible gentlemen, but the one whom she prefers, Valentine, does not have her father's approval. Having been foiled in her attempt to elope with her lover, she is appalled at the behavior of his closest friend, who claims to love her. In the end, she is united with Valentine, whose bravery has impressed the Duke.

Duke of Milan

A conventional nobleman; the Duke tries to protect the interests of his daughter by securing the most favorable husband possible for her. Ultimately, their choices coincide.

Thurio

This foolish rival to Valentine loses the Duke's favor at the end of the play, when he is quick to relinquish his claim to Silvia.

Eglamour

Another of Silvia's suitors, Eglamour is sympathetic in that he aids her in her escape from Milan in pursuit of Valentine.

Speed

Valentine's witty servant; he takes great pleasure in aggravating his master. Together with Launce, he offers a comic reflection of the concerns of the main characters.

Launce

Proteus's servant; he functions exactly as Speed. The character is justly famous for his monologues on the subject of his ungrateful, ill-behaved dog, Crab.

Lucetta

Julia's waiting woman; she acts as a sounding board for her mistress's emotions in the early part of the play, coaxing her along to recognize the direction of her affections and, at the same time, playfully teasing her about her feelings.

SUMMARIES AND COMMENTARIES

ACT I – SCENE 1

Summary

The scene is Verona, where two well-born young friends, Valentine and Proteus, are taking leave of one another. "He after honour hunts, I after love" says Proteus, once Valentine has departed for Milan. The latter's efforts to persuade his friend to travel abroad with him have failed. He warned of love's caprices: "One fading moment's mirth [is bought]/With twenty watchful, weary, tedious nights," and Proteus countered that love has a way of capturing even its cleverest detractors:

> Yet writers say, as in the sweetest bud
> The eating canker [worm] dwells, so eating love
> Inhabits in the finest wits of all.
>
> (42-44)

Proteus had sent Valentine's "clownish servant" to deliver a missive to his love, Julia, which Speed, as he is called, now reports on. The two banter for a short time before Proteus learns that his mistress acted "as hard as steel." "Henceforth carry your letters yourself," the irritated servant exclaims as he exits.

Commentary

The first scene prepares a very conventional thematic contrast, one between the young man who boasts of his independence and seeks adventure as his "future hope," and the one who is hopelessly in love. Further, the background for a conflict between friendship and love is provided. Shakespeare was, no doubt, aware of numerous contemporary Romances, many adapted from Italian sources, which dealt with similar themes and materials. The conflict between loyalties of kinship, friendship, and love preoccupied him elsewhere too, notably in his sonnets and in another "Verona" play, *Romeo and Juliet*. Important in the opening dialogue is the tone of cheerful antagonism, two good friends "twitting" one another, rather than any serious debating between the two.

Shakespeare dramatically demonstrates Proteus's frustration by having Speed draw out the anxiously awaited "news" from Julia. By the end of the scene, Proteus bids him to be hanged ("destined to a drier death") for "failing" in his role as go-between. Typical of the exchanges between the two is the following, which draws on the stock "sylvan" imagery of Romantic tales for its comedy:

> *Speed:* The shepherd seeks the sheep, and not the sheep the shepherd; but I seek my master, and my master seeks not me. Therefore I am no sheep.
> *Proteus:* The sheep for fodder follow the shepherd; the shepherd for food follows not the sheep; thou for wages followest thy master; thy master for wages follows not thee. Therefore thou art a sheep.
> *Speed:* Such another proof will make me cry "baa."
>
> (89-96)

ACT I–SCENE 2

Summary

Julia asks her "waiting woman," Lucetta, if she "counsels" her "to fall in love," after which the servant appraises the eligible suitors named by her mistress. Sir Eglamour is "well-spoken, neat, and fine," Mercatio is wealthy, but Proteus is most favored. Asked to explain why, Lucetta responds:

> I have no other but a woman's reason:
> I think him so because I think him so.

> (23-24)

Julia apparently grows angry with Lucetta when she learns of Proteus's letter:

> Dare you presume to harbour wanton lines?
> To whisper and conspire against my youth?

> (42-43)

But with Lucetta out of the room, she has second thoughts, and she calls after her to return with the letter. The scene ends as Julia tears the letter to shreds, only desperately to try piecing it together again. The servant wryly tells her mistress that she knows exactly what is going on: "I see things too, although you judge I wink" [have my eyes shut].

Commentary

The scene is structured around Julia's two solo passages on stage. In the first, she wrestles with her feelings in the after-flush of excitement, having learned that the man who most occupies her thoughts has just sent his regards through a messenger. Lucetta, who certainly timed her revelation to achieve full shock effect on the tender Julia, must secretly be amused at her mistress's wild overreaction. The "real" feelings emerge when Julia is alone: "Inward joy enforced my heart to smile."

Shakespeare has crafted the scene in such a way to allow maximum pleasure for the audience at Julia's pleasant/unpleasant consternation. Notice the way she pulls herself together, playing the part (not very well) of perfect indifference when she bids Lucetta to return. "What would your ladyship?" asks the servant, holding back her amusement. Julia tries small talk: "Is it near dinnertime?" she asks, but Lucetta is not fooled. When Julia tears up the letter, it is with much the same frustration (and false indifference) that Proteus showed in the previous scene.

Alone on stage a second time, Julia gushes with emotion, toying with the scraps of shredded paper as if they were doll-like representatives of herself and her lover: "Poor forlorn Proteus," she reads, "passionate Proteus,/To the sweet Julia":

> That I'll tear away. —
> And yet I will not, sith so prettily
> He couples it to his complaining names.
> Thus will I fold them one upon another.
> Now kiss, embrace, contend, do what you will.
>
> (125-29)

In this short scene, one gets a glimpse of the type of heroine Shakespeare was to enhance in charm and complexity in his future comedies.

ACT I – SCENE 3

Summary

Proteus's father decides to send his son abroad to Milan, where Valentine has gone, to gain experience of the world. When Proteus comes onto the stage, he is obviously in a daydream, clutching a love letter and warbling ("O heavenly Julia") in such a way as to make his father even more determined to "make a man of him." Proteus lies about the letter, saying it is from Valentine. Antonio will not listen to his son's plea for a short reprieve to prepare for his trip: "For what I will, I will, and there an end."

Commentary

Fathers traditionally block the paths of lovers in romantic comedy, and so it is at this moment of *The Two Gentlemen of Verona*. The blow to Proteus, however, spurs him to utter some of the finest lines of poetry in the play:

> O, how this spring of love resembleth
> The uncertain glory of an April day,
> Which now shows all the beauty of the sun,
> And by and by a cloud takes all away!
>
> (84-87)

ACT II – SCENE 1

Summary

In Milan, we find Speed taking great pleasure in aggravating his master, who shows all the external signs of being in love. "You have learned," he tells Valentine,

> to wreathe your arms, like a malcontent; to
> relish a lovesong, like a robin redbreast;
> to walk alone, like one that had the pestilence;
> to sigh, like a schoolboy that had lost his A B C. . . .
>
> (18-21)

When the object of his affections requests the letter she had commissioned him to write for her to a "third party," it is obvious to Speed that the love letter was really meant for Valentine himself, an indirect expression of affection from Silvia. Valentine, however, does not seem to catch on. The previous words exchanged with Speed are all too appropriate:

> *Speed:*   If you love her, you cannot see her.
> *Valentine:* Why?
> *Speed:*   Because Love is blind.
>
> (74-76)

Speed turns the talk to more practical matters, in the tradition of eternally hungry comic servants, "though the chamelon Love can feed on the air, I am one that am nourished by my victuals, and would fain have meat," and the two exit.

Commentary

With quick, almost too obvious irony, Valentine has fallen in love. Silvia is well worth the fall, it seems, as she cleverly "woos [him] by a figure," as Speed puts it. "Eating love" has indeed begun to take possession of this "fine wit" Valentine. In Speed's delineation of lovers' affectations, Shakespeare pokes gentle fun at youthful folly.

ACT II — SCENES 2 and 3

Summary

Julia gives Proteus a ring to remember her by as he prepares to depart by ship for Milan. Forcing back tears, they say goodbye:

> *Proteus:* The tide is now — nay, not thy tide of tears;
> That tide will stay me longer than I should.
> (14-15)

Proteus's servant, Launce, also suffers an emotional separation too — from his ungrateful dog, Crab. Launce's sentimentality is congenital, it seems: "all the kind of the Launces have this very fault." This makes him all the more upset at his dog's stiff upper lip:

> My mother weeping, my father wailing,
> my sister crying, our maid howling, our
> cat wringing her hands, and all our house in
> a great perplexity, yet did not this cruel-hearted
> cur shed one tear.
> (6-10)

Commentary

Shakespeare's genius in his greatest plays resides in his ability to straddle the range of human experience like some colossus. In sharply contrasting scenes, he evokes the complexity of life and love and death and hate. When Hamlet is on the way to his inevitable demise, Shakespeare introduces a clownish/wise gravedigger who jauntily philosophizes, unearthed skull in hand. Nothing approaching the same effect is achieved in *The Two Gentlemen of Verona*; however, the simple technique of juxtaposing contrasting moods within a single human experience (leave-taking) is comparable, and typical of Shakespearean playwriting. Launce's hilarious bellowing acts as a gloss on the bittersweet parting of Julia and Proteus.

ACT II – SCENE 4

Summary

At Silvia's instigation, two of her suitors, Thurio and Valentine, engage in verbal fisticuffs to cull her favor. The level of debate is not particularly high:

> *Silvia:* What, angry, Sir Thurio! Do you change color!
> *Valentine:* Give him leave, Madam; he is a kind of chameleon.
> *Thurio:* That hath more mind to feed on your blood than live in your air.
>
> (23-25)

Silvia's father interrupts the proceedings to tell them of the unexpected arrival of Sir Proteus; he is assured of Proteus's upstanding good character by Valentine:

> He is complete in feature and in mind
> With all good grace to grace a gentleman.
>
> (73-74)

Hardly has he finished when Proteus comes onto the stage and is warmly greeted by his friend, who introduces him to Silvia. Proteus greets her with conventional good manners, telling her that he is "too mean a servant/To have a look of such a worthy mistress." When Silvia exits, Valentine inquires after friends and relations in Verona, including Julia. Proteus soon learns that his friend has fallen in love with Silvia:

> *Proteus:* Enough; I read your fortune in your eye.
> Was this the idol that you worship so?
> *Valentine:* Even she; and is she not a heavenly saint?
> *Proteus:* No, but she is an earthly paragon.
>
> (143-46)

He further learns of their betrothal and that Valentine is troubled by a wealthy rival.

Left alone, Proteus reveals in a monologue his own infatuation with Silvia, something he feels to such an extent that his love for Julia,

> . . . like a waxen image 'gainst a fire,
> Bears no impression of the thing it was.
>
> (201-2)

The scene ends on his somewhat shocking remark:

> If I can check my erring love, I will;
> If not, to compass [win] her I'll use my skill.
>
> (213-14)

Commentary

The entire scene would be quite ordinary, if not downright dull, if it weren't for the fact that we know by Proteus's last lines that once he meets Silvia a strange and ambiguous undercurrent colors the action and dialogue. The usually matter-of-fact Valentine asks Proteus about Julia, but, with love of Silvia *very much* on his mind, Proteus tries to change the subject: "I know you joy not in a love discourse." Then later, when the two friends argue the relative merits of their ladies—standard behavior for friends—Proteus becomes quite abrupt:

> *Proteus:* Why, Valentine, what braggardism is this?
> *Valentine:* Pardon me, Proteus. All I can is nothing
> To her, whose worth makes other worthies
> nothing;
> She is alone.
> *Proteus:* Then let her alone.
> *Valentine:* Not for the world.
>
> (164-69)

Shakespeare, like others before him, uses the idea of "love at first sight" to stir the ashes of a dying plot, and, here, he manufactures an inner conflict to enhance the character of Proteus.

> Methinks my zeal to Valentine is cold,
> And that I love him not as I was wont.
> O, but I love his lady too too much!
>
> (203-5)

ACT II – SCENES 5 and 6

Summary

Speed welcomes Launce to Padua. (Since they are in Milan he may be teasing the other servant, taking him for a fool.) Speed inquires "how did thy master part with Madam Julia?" The two then bandy the topic about in the customary lewd fashion for "low" characters:

> *Launce:* Marry, thus: when it stands well with him,
> it stands well with her,
>
> (22-23)

but the gist of Launce's remarks affirms that Proteus and Julia are virtually married.

Scene six consists of a forty-three-line monologue in which Proteus resolves to betray Julia and Valentine in pursuit of Silvia. To start, he will inform Silvia's father that the couple are planning to elope: "All enraged, he [the father] will banish Valentine." After that, outwitting Thurio should be no problem.

Commentary

What shocks the audience (and often upsets critics) is the quickness with which Proteus translates infatuation with Silvia into concrete plans to jilt his betrothed and betray his closest friend. The scene between Launce and Speed serves to emphasize the effect: no sooner has Launce reaffirmed his master's commitment to Julia, than Proteus dismisses her as "a twinkling star" compared to Silvia, "a celestial sun." His rationalization is similar to the intellectual sleight of hand in *Love's Labour's Lost* with the difference that, here, deep personal bonds are being violated:

> I cannot leave to love, and yet I do;
> But there I leave to love where I should love.
> Julia I lose, and Valentine I lose.
> If I keep them, I needs must lose myself;
> If I lose them, thus find I by their loss

> For Valentine, myself; for Julia, Silvia.
> I to myself am dearer than a friend. . . .
>
> (18-24)

As will be the case with the great "villains" Shakespeare is yet to create, Proteus's argument hinges on egotism, placing "self" above the sacred demands of friendship.

ACT II – SCENE 7

Summary

Julia asks Lucetta's advice once again:

> How, with my honor, I may undertake
> A journey to my loving Proteus?
>
> (6-7)

Lucetta's counsel is conventional, and in such comedies conventionally ignored by her mistress:

> I do not seek to quench your love's hot fire,
> But qualify the fire's extreme rage,
> Lest it should burn above the bounds of reason.
>
> (21-23)

"The more thou damm'st it up, the more it burns," Julia replies. Julia plans to disguise herself as "some well-reputed page" and to travel to Milan at once.

Commentary

Shakespeare provides this glimpse of the innocent and loving Julia while Proteus's treacherous words still echo in our ears from the previous scene. There is something touching in her speech as she compares her love to the movement of a stream:

> The current that with gentle murmur glides,
> Thou know'st, being stopped, impatiently doth rage;

But when his fair course is not hindered,
He makes sweet music with th' enameled stones,
Giving a gentle kiss to every sedge
He overtaketh in his pilgrimage;
And by so many winding nooks he strays,
With willing sport, to the wild ocean.

(25-32)

However, when Julia sings the praises of her lover later in the scene, Shakespeare seems to be hammering too hard at the point of innocence betrayed:

His words are bonds, his oaths are oracles;
His love sincere, his thoughts immaculate;
His tears pure messengers sent from his heart;
His heart as far from fraud as heaven from earth.

(75-78)

ACT III – SCENE 1

Summary

After Proteus betrays Valentine to the Duke ("Thus, for my duty's sake, I rather chose/To cross my friend in his intended drift"), the Duke fully satisfies himself that his daughter is indeed planning to elope with the Veronese gentleman instead of marrying the wealthy merchant, Thurio. He perpetrates a ruse on Valentine, pretending himself to be in love with a woman and asking advice on how best to gain her favor. Valentine falls for the trick, assuring the Duke,

That man that hath a tongue, I say, is no man,
If with his tongue he cannot win a woman.

(104-5)

Eager to please Silvia's father, Valentine cheerfully explains how best to conceal a rope ladder when approaching the tower where his lover is "imprisoned." The Duke opens Valentine's cloak to discover a love letter to Silvia *and* "an engine [ladder] fit for my proceeding." The upshot is instant banishment for the gullible Valentine, who is left to lament:

> And why not death rather than living torment?
> To die is to be banished from myself;
> And Silvia is myself.
>
> (170-72)

Proteus arrives with "comforting" words ("Time is the nurse and breeder of all good"). He suggests that Valentine accept banishment, satisfying himself with letters to Silvia, which Proteus promises to deliver:

> Thy letters may be here, though thou art hence;
> Which, being writ to me, shall be delivered
> Even in the milk-white bosom of thy love.
>
> (248-50)

To end the scene, Shakespeare has Speed and Launce discuss the merits of the latter's loved one, itemized on a sheet of paper which he carries with him.

Commentary

The dramatic interest in this scene resides in the protracted "entrapment" of Valentine. Rather than accuse him outright of secretly planning to run off with Silvia, the Duke pretends to seek advice from Valentine on how to snare a woman. Imagine the steady building of eagerness on Valentine's part (showing off to his "father-in-law"), coupled with the Duke's muted anger while, point for point, he proves to himself the truth of Proteus's accusation. The Duke described himself as ever "shunning rashness," hence the slow and deliberate method he employs. Once sure, however, he is severe:

> But if thou linger in my territories
> Longer than swiftest expedition
> Will give thee time to leave our royal court,
> By heaven, my wrath shall far exceed the love
> I ever bore my daughter or thyself.
>
> (163-67)

Themes from the main plot are then echoed by Launce and Speed. In a very long dialogue about the pros and cons of Launce's lady, the ultimate reason for the choice of this woman is no different from the Duke's preference for Thurio over Valentine as a suitor for Silvia: money. Launce takes the good with the bad, more often turning the bad into the good:

> *Speed* [reading from the list]:
>   "Item: she hath no teeth."
> *Launce:* I care not for that neither,
>   Because I love crusts.
>
> (244-46)

The rationalization can be explained by a later item:

> *Speed:* "Item: she hath more hair than wit,
>   and more faults than hairs,
>   and more wealth than faults."
> *Launce:* Stop there: I'll have her. She was mine,
>   and not mine, twice or thrice in that last article.
>
> (361-65)

All this time Launce has been delaying Speed from joining his master, for which he'll receive punishment. This minor "betrayal" parallels the knavery of his master:

> *Launce:* Now will he be swinged for reading my letter —
>   an unmannerly slave, that will thrust himself
>   into secrets! I'll after, to rejoice in the
>   boy's correction.
>
> (392-95)

ACT III – SCENE 2

Summary

Thurio has had a very difficult time of wooing Silvia since Valentine's banishment, so the Duke solicits Proteus's aid.

> *Duke:* What might we do to make the girl forget
>   The love of Valentine, and love Sir Thurio?

> *Proteus:* The best way is to slander Valentine
> With falsehood, cowardice, and poor descent,
> Three things that women highly hold in hate.
>
> (29-33)

Proteus himself will be the chief slanderer, since Silvia (described as being "lumpish, heavy, melancholy") is most likely to believe what Valentine's dear friend says. Proteus furthermore advises Sir Thurio to whet her desire "by wailful sonnets" and a "sweet consort" (hired musicians).

Commentary

Proteus's guile having completely duped the Duke and Sir Thurio, the audience must now be fascinated by the potential depths to which this one-time friend will sink in pursuit of his wild fancy. His proven success in wooing Julia serves him well as consultant to the luckless Sir Thurio:

> After your dire-lamenting elegies,
> Visit by night your lady's chamber window. . . .
>
> (82-83)

ACT IV – SCENES 1 and 2

Summary

Valentine and Speed are accosted by an honorable band of thieves who are so impressed by the travelers' noble demeanor that they not only spare their lives, but offer Valentine the generalship of their gang.

> By the bare scalp of Robin Hood's fat friar,
> This fellow were a king for our wild faction!
>
> (36-37)

The same outlaw who utters these words explains that his own crime amounted to no more than "practicing [planning] to steal away a lady." They claim to be gentlemen, and they urge Valentine to "make virtue of necessity"; otherwise, they'll kill him. He accepts.

In Milan, Proteus and Sir Thurio approach Silvia's dwelling at night. Proteus uses the excuse of giving aid to Thurio as a means to approach Silvia, who consistently spurns him:

> Yet, spaniel-like, the more she spurns my love,
> The more it grows, and fawneth on her still.
>
> (14-15)

Disguised as a boy and fresh from Verona, Julia comes upon the scene of Proteus singing a love song outside of Silvia's window. Thurio departs after the song, and Julia watches as her lover declares his feelings for another woman. He even goes so far as to say that she, Julia, is dead.

Commentary

Even the thieves instinctively recognize the nobility of the banished Valentine, in the "romantic" tradition of true quality being evident to all:

> . . . seeing you are beautified
> With goodly shape, and by your own report
> A linguist, and a man of such perfection
> As we do in our quality much want—
>
> (55-58)

Note the two earmarks of this high-minded gentleman: a) he rebukes Speed for being too anxious to save his skin by joining the brigands; b) he joins on condition that, under his governance, the band shall neither rob poor people, nor fall upon "silly [defenseless] women." In a later play, *Henry IV, Part 1*, Shakespeare was to take this whole tradition of "noble brigandry" and turn it on its head in the persons of fat Jack Falstaff and his sleazy crew. In *The Two Gentlemen of Verona*, the thieves are purely and simply a part of the romantic staple of the Elizabethans' favorite reading. A modern director would be hard put not to play the scene as parody.

Probably one of the most poignant scenes in the play is the one depicting the exhausted, lovelorn Julia, dressed as a page, as she catches the first glimpse of Proteus. In order to preserve her disguise, she cannot reveal the hurt she must be experiencing as she listens to Proteus sing a love song to Silvia.

> *Host:* How now! Are you sadder than you were before?
> How do you, man? The music likes you not.
> *Julia:* You mistake; the musician likes me not.
> *Host:* Why, my pretty youth?
> *Julia:* He plays false, father.
> *Host:* How? Out of tune on the strings?
> *Julia:* Not so; but yet so false that he grieves my very heart-
> strings.

> (55-61)

Towards the end of the scene, Silvia seems to be faltering slightly, as she consents to give Proteus a picture of herself. One wonders if this same device were part of the process whereby he had won Julia's heart. After calling Proteus a "subtle, perjured, false, disloyal man," she consents to give the picture, rationalizing thus:

> I am very loath to be your idol, sir;
> But since your falsehood shall become you well
> To worship shadows and adore false shapes,
> Send to me in the morning, and I'll send it.

> (128-31)

Julia surely notices the apparent minor capitulation, as she remarks,

> . . . it hath been the longest night
> That e'er I watched, and the most heaviest.

> (140-41)

ACT IV – SCENES 3 and 4

Summary

Silvia entreats Eglamour to accompany her to Mantua, where Valentine is currently living. Eglamour has suffered a loss in love himself (his "true love died"), so he is touched when Silvia bids him "think upon my grief, a lady's grief." They are to meet in the evening at Friar Patrick's cell, where Silvia "intend[s] holy confession," and whence they shall depart.

Launce berates his dog, Crab, for ungentlemanly behavior. Crab stole a capon's leg from Lady Silvia's plate, then he relieved himself unashamedly under the Duke's table. To save his dog's hide, Launce took the blame, *and* the whipping:

> If I had not had more wit than he, to take a
> fault upon me that he did, I think verily
> he had been hanged for it.
>
> (14-16)

"How many masters would do this for his servant?" Launce asks his dog. Certainly not Proteus, as we now learn. He scolds Launce for making the absurd mistake of offering his own dog as a gift to Silvia after the one Proteus meant for her had been stolen. From the sound of it, Launce seems to have substituted a Great Dane for a small poodle on the logical grounds that his dog is "as big as ten of yours, and therefore [is] the gift the greater."

Proteus has taken on a page (Julia in disguise) to help him pursue Silvia. He tells her to deliver a ring in exchange for the promised picture, whereupon Julia is hard put to contain her feelings. Queried about her reaction, she says of the absent mistress (really herself):

> She dreams on him that hath forgot her love;
> You dote on her that cares not for your love.
> 'Tis pity love should be so contrary;
> And thinking on it makes me cry, "Alas!"
>
> (86-89)

In the last part of the scene, Julia delivers the ring (in fact, the one Julia had given Proteus as a keepsake) to Silvia, who is appalled at the gift.

> For I have heard him say a thousand times
> His Julia gave it him at his departure.
>
> (139-40)

Julia nearly reveals herself under the pressure.

> *Silvia:* Dost thou know her?
> *Julia:* Almost as well as I do know myself.
> To think upon her woes, I do protest
> That I have wept a hundred several times.
>
> (147-50)

Left with the picture of her sympathetic rival, Julia laments the absurdity of her situation. She envies the "senseless form" (inert picture) that shall "be worshipped, kissed, loved, and adored."

Commentary

In these scenes, we have two instances of behavior in counterpoint to Proteus's, one serious and one comic. Eglamour is not so much a character in his own right as he is a means to further the plot and to represent an example of noble, selfless behavior. Launce is, of course, the comic equivalent of this altruism, a true friend to his dog:

> I have set in the stocks for puddings [sausages]
> he hath stol'n; otherwise he had been executed.
> I have stood on the pillory for geese he hath killed;
> otherwise he had suffered for it.
>
> (33-36)

In the scenes between Julia (as page) and Proteus, then Julia and Silvia, Shakespeare comes as close as he does anywhere in *The Two Gentlemen of Verona* to creating the dramatic intensity which his later romantic comedies are noted for. The disguise motif functions here similarly to its later uses—in *As You Like It* or *Twelfth Night*, the difference being the poetic fabric is not quite of the same quality. Note the tension as Proteus unknowingly insults his lover to her face:

> *Proteus:* . . . go presently, and take this ring with thee;
> Deliver it to Madam Silvia.
> She loved me well delivered it to me.
> *Julia:* It seems you loved not her, to leave her token.
> She is dead, belike?
> *Proteus:* Not so; I think she lives.
> *Julia:* Alas!
> *Proteus:* Why dost thou cry "alas"?

Julia: I cannot choose
             But pity her.

(76-85)

Julia's conundrum worsens as she meets her arch-rival and finds her not at all unpleasant: "A virtuous gentlewoman, mild and beautiful!" There is special poignance in the concluding monologue, as Julia contemplates the image of her rival, by turns mildly disparaging her qualities ("and yet the painter flattered her a little") and venting her inner anger:

I'll use thee [the picture] kindly for thy mistress' sake,
That used me so; or else, by Jove I vow,
I should have scratched out your unseeing eyes,
To make my master out of love with thee!

(207-10)

The idea of giving Julia the stage property image to address in her moment of despair adds a concreteness to the scene. Note the different ways in which the actress playing Julia might handle the portrait.

ACT V – SCENES 1, 2, and 3

Summary

Eglamour and Silvia flee to the forest, where she is captured by the outlaws. As they take her away to their captain (Valentine), she exclaims: "O Valentine, this I endure for thee." Meantime, a session in which Proteus advises Thurio on his progress with Silvia is interrupted by the Duke, who tells them of Eglamour and Silvia's flight. They exist separately.

Proteus: And I will follow more for Silvia's love
           Than hate of Eglamour, that goes with her.
Julia: And I will follow, more to cross that love
           Than hate for Silvia, that is gone for love.

(53-56)

Commentary

Shakespeare speeds up the plot by his usual technique of quickly interchanging scenes. The three here, a) Silvia fleeing; b) the Duke and others pursuing them; and c) Silvia's capture by outlaws, take up roughly seventy lines. The pleasant irony of Silvia's last "despairing" line is obvious, as is much in this romantic tale.

ACT V – SCENE 4

Summary

A solitary Valentine muses on his present condition:

> Here can I sit alone, unseen of any,
> And to the nightingale's complaining notes
> Tune my distresses and record my woes.
>
> (4-6)

Abruptly interrupted by the spectacle of his friend Proteus in hot pursuit of Silvia, Valentine doubts his very senses: "How like a dream is this I see and hear!" Valentine remains mute until the moment when Proteus threatens violence.

> | Proteus: | In love, |
> | | Who respects friend? |
> | Silvia: | All men but Proteus. |
> | Proteus: | Nay, if the gentle spirit of moving words |
> | | Can no way change you to a milder form, |
> | | I'll woo you like a soldier, at arms' end, |
> | | And love you 'gainst the nature of love, – force ye. |
> | Silvia: | O heaven! |
> | Proteus: | I'll force thee yield to my desire. |
> | Valentine: | Ruffian, let go that rude uncivil touch, |
> | | Thou friend of an ill fashion! |
>
> (53-63)

Confronted by his friend, Proteus apologizes and is forgiven at once by Valentine. Silvia remains silent. When Julia faints, trying to cover up her emotional turmoil by telling Proteus that she (as page) was upset at not delivering the ring to Silvia as promised, it is discovered that she is indeed Proteus's former lover. She hands him the wrong ring, the one he had given *her* as a keepsake. The two reconcile.

When Thurio is confronted by an angry Valentine, he gives up claim to Silvia, causing the Duke to change heart:

> I do applaud thy spirit, Valentine,
> And think thee worthy of an empress' love.
>
> (140-41)

Valentine accepts and asks the Duke to "grant one boon," a general amnesty for the band of gentlemen-thieves he has been leading these past months. That done, all retire to soothe the bad feelings "with triumphs, mirth, and rare solemnity."

Commentary

In terms of plausibility, the last scene of *The Two Gentlemen of Verona* leaves much to be desired. The rapid movement from pastoral melancholy to high melodrama to festive comedy, ending in a pair of marriages needs to be accepted in the spirit of a fairy tale, where logic and consistent human motivation are irrelevant. Consider Silvia. She is nearly raped, then instants later, she sees her husband-to-be embracing her attacker as an eternal friend. No questions are asked, and significantly she has not a single line after her desperate line, "O heaven!" And Julia's easy acceptance of the perfidious Proteus seems almost as odd at the end of this comedy. The conventions of romance prevail, as the thieves gain pardons and a marriage banquet is announced. Valentine's proposed "punishment" for Proteus, at the end of the scene, seems feeble:

> Come Proteus; 'tis your penance but to hear
> The story of your loves discovered.
>
> (170-71)

In some of Shakespeare's later comedies there are "dark" moments, as we find here (*e.g.*, the intrigue and punishment of Malvolio in *Twelfth Night*), but they are integrated more fully into the main action, and not, as one gets the impression in *The Two Gentlemen of Verona*, "dashed off" to complete the plot.

SELECTED BIBLIOGRAPHY

ADAMS, J. Q. *A Life of William Shakespeare.* Boston: Houghton Mifflin Co., 1923.

ALEXANDER, PETER. *Shakespeare.* Oxford: Oxford University Press, 1964.

BEVINGTON, DAVID. *Shakespeare.* Arlington Heights, Ill.: A.H.M. Publications, 1978.

BLOOM, EDWARD A., ed. *Shakespeare 1564-1964.* Providence: Brown University Press, 1964.

BRADLEY, A. C. *Shakespearean Tragedy.* London: The Macmillan Co., 1904.

CHARLTON, H. B. *Shakespearean Tragedy.* Cambridge, England: Cambridge University Press, 1948.

CRAIG, HARDIN. "The Great Trio," *An Interpretation of Shakespeare.* Columbia, Missouri: Lucas Brothers, 1966.

FARNHAM, WILLARD. *The Medieval Heritage of Elizabethan Tragedy.* Berkeley, California: University of California Press, 1936.

GIBSON, H. N. *The Shakespeare Claimants.* New York: Barnes & Noble, Inc., 1962.

HEILMAN, ROBERT B. *Magic in the Web.* Lexington, Kentucky: University of Kentucky Press, 1956.

KNIGHT, G. WILSON. *The Wheel of Fire.* London: Oxford University Press, 1930.

LEAVIS, F. R. *The Common Pursuit.* Hardmonsworth, Middlesex: Penguin Books, Ltd., 1963.

RIBNER, IRVING. *Patterns in Shakespearean Tragedy.* New York: Barnes & Noble, Inc., 1960.

SEWELL, ARTHUR. *Character and Society in Shakespeare.* Oxford: Clarendon Press, 1951.

SPIVACK, BERNARD. *Shakespeare and the Allegory of Evil.* New York: Columbia University Press, 1958.

STIRLING, BRENTS. *Unity in Shakespearean Tragedy: The Interplay of Theme and Character.* New York: Columbia University Press, 1956.